The Discipline Framework

Unlock Your Potential
Through Daily Action

Diana Weber

Chapter 1: The Foundation of Discipline

Understanding the Psychology of Self Control

Self-control, at its core, is the ability to regulate one's thoughts, emotions, and behaviors in the face of temptations or impulses. It is the silent force steering decisions, the internal compass that determines whether we succumb to immediate gratification or resist in pursuit of long-term goals. To understand its essence, one must first unravel the intricate web of the human psyche, where self-control operates. It is not merely an innate trait but a skill that can be cultivated with intention and practice.

The foundation of self-control lies in the human brain, particularly in the prefrontal cortex. This part of the brain, responsible for executive functions such as planning, decision-making, and impulse regulation, acts as the command center for self-control. It is here that the tug-of-war between immediate desires and long-term aspirations unfolds. When the prefrontal cortex is functioning optimally, it allows individuals to pause, evaluate their options, and make choices aligned with their goals. However, this process is far from automatic and requires a conscious effort to override the primal instincts of the brain's limbic system, which craves instant rewards.

One of the most fascinating aspects of self-control is its finite nature. Research has shown that self-control operates much like a muscle—it can be strengthened over time but also fatigued with overuse. This phenomenon, known as ego depletion, suggests that the more self-control one exerts in a given period, the less one has available for subsequent tasks. For example, resisting the temptation to indulge in junk food might leave an individual less equipped to focus on a demanding work assignment later in the day. Understanding this limitation is crucial, as it underscores the importance of managing one's energy and environment to minimize unnecessary self-control exertion.

The environment plays a pivotal role in shaping self-control. Temptations are often external stimuli—sweets on a kitchen counter, notifications on a smartphone, or the lure of binge-worthy television shows. By modifying one's surroundings to reduce exposure to these triggers, the need for self-control diminishes. This concept, known as situational self-control, emphasizes the importance of proactive measures. For instance, keeping unhealthy snacks out of sight or scheduling specific times to check emails can significantly enhance one's ability to stay on track.

Equally important is the role of identity in self-control. Individuals who perceive themselves as disciplined or goal-oriented are more likely to exhibit self-control behaviors. This is because actions are often aligned with self-perception. If someone identifies as a healthy eater, they are less likely to indulge in unhealthy foods, as doing so would conflict with their self-image. Cultivating an identity that supports one's goals can be a powerful tool in enhancing self-control.

Emotions add another layer of complexity to the psychology of self-control. Stress, anxiety, and frustration can weaken the prefrontal cortex's ability to regulate impulses, making it more challenging to resist temptations. This is why individuals often turn to comfort foods or procrastination during times of emotional distress. Developing emotional regulation skills, such as mindfulness, deep breathing, or journaling, can help mitigate the impact of negative emotions on self-control. By addressing the root cause of emotional triggers, individuals can create a more stable foundation for self-regulation.

Goal clarity serves as a beacon for self-control. When goals are vague or ambiguous, the brain struggles to prioritize actions, leading to indecision and susceptibility to distractions. Clear, specific, and measurable goals provide a roadmap for the brain, making it easier to resist temptations that deviate from the desired path. For instance, the goal of "exercising three times a week for 30 minutes" is far more actionable than a vague intention to "get fit." The former provides a concrete framework that the mind can follow, reducing the cognitive load required for self-control.

Another critical factor is the interplay between motivation and self-control. While self-control focuses on resisting impulses, motivation is the driving force that propels individuals toward their goals. The two are closely intertwined, as high levels of motivation can enhance self-control by providing a compelling reason to stay disciplined. Conversely, a lack of motivation can undermine self-control, as the brain struggles to justify the effort required to resist temptations. Intrinsic motivation, which stems from internal desires and values, is particularly effective in sustaining self-control over the long term.

The role of habits cannot be overstated in the realm of self-control. Habits are the brain's way of automating repetitive actions, conserving mental energy for more complex tasks. When a behavior becomes habitual, it requires minimal self-control to execute. For instance, brushing your teeth before bed is likely a habit that requires little to no conscious effort. By consciously cultivating positive habits, individuals can reduce the reliance on self-control for daily routines, freeing up mental resources for more demanding challenges.

Self-compassion emerges as a surprising ally in the journey of mastering self-control. Contrary to the belief that harsh self-criticism fosters discipline, studies have shown that individuals who practice self-compassion are more likely to exhibit self-control. This is because self-compassion reduces the emotional toll of setbacks, allowing individuals to recover and refocus more effectively. Viewing lapses in self-control as opportunities for growth rather than failures fosters resilience and a long-term commitment to one's goals.

The psychology of self-control also highlights the importance of delayed gratification. The ability to postpone immediate rewards in favor of long-term benefits is a hallmark of self-regulation. The famous "Marshmallow Test," conducted by psychologist Walter Mischel, demonstrated that children who could delay gratification were more likely to achieve success later in life. This ability to wait is not merely a matter of willpower but a skill that can be honed through practice. Techniques such as visualization, where individuals imagine the future benefits of their actions, can enhance the capacity for delayed gratification.

Social influences significantly impact self-control as well. The people with whom one interacts can either strengthen or weaken self-regulation. Surrounding oneself with individuals who share similar goals or exhibit high levels of self-control can create a supportive environment that fosters discipline. Conversely, spending time with those who indulge in behaviors contrary to one's objectives can erode self-control. Building a network of accountability partners or mentors can provide the encouragement and guidance needed to stay on track.

Finally, the concept of self-control as a renewable resource offers a hopeful perspective. While ego depletion suggests that self-control can be temporarily exhausted, it is also true that it can be replenished through rest, proper nutrition, and activities that restore mental energy. Practices such as meditation, spending time in nature, or engaging in hobbies can recharge the prefrontal cortex, enhancing its capacity for self-regulation.

The Role of Habits in Shaping Success

Habits are the unseen architects of human behavior, quietly shaping the trajectory of lives with every repeated action. They are the small, consistent routines that, when compounded over time, determine whether an individual moves closer to their goals or drifts away from them. Success is not the result of monumental efforts made sporadically but rather the outcome of deliberate actions embedded into daily life. To understand the role of habits in shaping success, it is essential to delve into their mechanics, their formation, and the transformative power they hold.

At their core, habits are automatic behaviors triggered by specific cues in the environment. They are the brain's way of conserving energy by streamlining repetitive tasks. This automation frees up mental resources for more complex decision-making, allowing individuals to focus on creative or challenging endeavors without being bogged down by mundane choices. The habit loop—a concept popularized by Charles Duhigg in his work on the science of habits—explains how habits function in a cycle of cue, routine, and reward. For instance, the sight of a messy desk (cue) might prompt someone to organize their workspace (routine), resulting in a sense of accomplishment (reward). Over time, this sequence becomes ingrained, requiring little conscious effort to execute.

The power of habits lies in their cumulative effect. While a single action may seem insignificant, its repetition over weeks, months, or years can lead to profound changes. Consider a person who commits to reading just ten pages of a book each day. In isolation, ten pages may not seem like much, but over the course of a year, this small habit translates to reading over 3,600 pages—equivalent to roughly 12 books. Similarly, saving a modest amount of money each week can lead to substantial financial reserves over time. These examples illustrate how habits compound, turning small daily actions into significant achievements.

The process of habit formation is both a science and an art. Psychologists suggest that it takes an average of 66 days for a new behavior to become automatic, though this timeline can vary depending on the complexity of the habit and the individual's consistency. The key to successful habit formation lies in starting small and focusing on incremental progress. Attempting to overhaul one's life overnight by adopting numerous habits simultaneously often leads to burnout and frustration. Instead, beginning with a single, manageable habit—such as drinking a glass of water upon waking—builds confidence and creates a foundation for future changes.

The environment plays a crucial role in shaping habits. People are products of their surroundings, and their behaviors are often influenced by the cues and triggers in their environment. For example, a person who keeps healthy snacks visible on their kitchen counter is more likely to make nutritious choices than someone whose counter is cluttered with sugary treats. By designing an environment that supports desired habits and minimizes exposure to temptations, individuals can make positive behaviors easier to adopt and sustain. This concept, known as environmental design, underscores the importance of intentionality in creating spaces that align with one's goals.

Accountability and social influence further enhance the likelihood of habit formation. When individuals share their goals with others or involve themselves in communities that support similar aspirations, they are more likely to stay committed to their habits. The presence of accountability partners or role models provides encouragement and reinforces the belief that success is achievable. For instance, someone striving to establish a regular exercise routine might find it easier to stay consistent by joining a fitness group or partnering with a friend who shares the same objective. The collective energy of a supportive community can amplify motivation and foster a sense of belonging, making the pursuit of habits more enjoyable.

One of the most significant challenges in habit formation is overcoming the initial resistance. The early stages of adopting a new habit often feel uncomfortable, as the brain resists change and clings to familiar routines. This resistance is rooted in the brain's preference for efficiency; breaking old patterns and establishing new ones requires effort and disrupts the status quo. To navigate this phase, it is essential to focus on the "why" behind the habit—understanding the deeper purpose or benefit it serves. For example, someone striving to wake up earlier might remind themselves of the extra time it provides to work on personal projects or enjoy a peaceful morning routine. Anchoring habits to meaningful goals creates a sense of purpose that motivates individuals to push through discomfort.

Momentum is another critical factor in sustaining habits. Once a habit is established, it creates a ripple effect, making it easier to adopt additional positive behaviors. This phenomenon, known as the "keystone habit effect," occurs when one habit sets off a chain reaction that influences other areas of life. For instance, committing to regular exercise often leads to improved sleep, healthier eating, and increased productivity. Identifying and focusing on keystone habits—those that have the greatest impact—can accelerate progress and create a foundation for holistic success.

Tracking and measuring progress are invaluable tools in habit formation. Keeping a record of daily actions provides a tangible sense of achievement and reinforces the behavior. Whether through a journal, a checklist, or a digital app, tracking habits creates a visual representation of consistency, which can be highly motivating. Moreover, reviewing progress allows individuals to identify patterns, celebrate milestones, and make adjustments as needed. This practice transforms habit formation into an intentional and reflective process, ensuring that efforts remain aligned with overarching goals.

While habits have the power to drive success, it is equally important to recognize and address detrimental habits that hinder progress. Negative habits, such as procrastination, excessive screen time, or unhealthy eating, often operate on the same cue-routine-reward loop as positive habits. The key to breaking these patterns lies in disrupting the cycle and replacing harmful routines with constructive alternatives. For example, someone who habitually checks their phone during work hours might replace this behavior with a short walk or a mindfulness exercise. By identifying the underlying cues and rewards associated with negative habits, individuals can rewire their behaviors and reclaim control over their actions.

Self-compassion plays a vital role in the journey of habit formation. It is natural to encounter setbacks, miss a day, or falter in the pursuit of consistency. Rather than succumbing to guilt or self-criticism, approaching these moments with understanding and a commitment to refocus fosters resilience. A single lapse does not negate progress; what matters is the ability to recover and continue moving forward. Viewing habit formation as a long-term process rather than a rigid standard allows for flexibility and adaptability, ensuring sustained growth over time.

Chapter 2: The Science Behind Daily Action

Why Small Steps Lead to Big Changes

Change often feels daunting. The gap between where you are and where you want to be can seem insurmountable, like staring up at the peak of a distant mountain. However, the secret to making meaningful progress isn't leaping to the summit in one bound but breaking the journey into manageable, consistent steps. Small actions, repeated over time, have the power to create monumental transformations. This principle is not only actionable but deeply rooted in human psychology, biology, and the laws of progress. behavior is naturally resistant to sudden, drastic change. The brain, in its quest to conserve energy, prefers routines and familiar patterns. When faced with large, overwhelming goals, the mind often responds with avoidance or procrastination. This is why ambitious resolutions—like losing fifty pounds, writing a novel, or saving an enormous sum of money—often fizzle out after an initial burst of enthusiasm. The scale of the task feels too overwhelming, and without immediate results, motivation wanes. Small steps, however, bypass this psychological barrier. By focusing on incremental progress, you reduce mental resistance and allow your brain to adapt gradually to new behaviors.

Consider the compound effect, a concept that highlights how small, consistent actions accumulate over time to produce significant outcomes. A single penny doubled every day for thirty days results in over five million dollars. This example, often used to illustrate compounding in finance, applies equally to personal growth and goal achievement. Whether it's exercising for ten minutes a day, reading one page of a book, or saving a few dollars each week, these small efforts compound, creating momentum that transforms into larger achievements. The initial steps may seem insignificant, but their cumulative impact is extraordinary.

Momentum is a critical factor in the success of small steps. Once you begin taking action, no matter how small, you create a sense of movement. This momentum generates motivation, making it easier to continue. Psychologists often refer to this as the "progress principle." When you see evidence of progress, no matter how minor, it fuels a sense of achievement and encourages you to persist. For instance, crossing off a single task on a to-do list or noticing slight improvements in your fitness after a few short workouts can ignite a chain reaction of positive behaviors. Momentum builds confidence, and confidence sustains action.

Breaking tasks into small steps also enhances focus. The human brain struggles to maintain attention over extended periods or when faced with multifaceted challenges. Large goals tend to overwhelm, leading to decision fatigue and a loss of direction. By narrowing your focus to a single, achievable step, you eliminate unnecessary distractions and allow your mind to channel its energy effectively. This approach not only increases productivity but also reduces stress and anxiety. Completing one small action at a time creates a sense of control and clarity, enabling you to stay on track without feeling overwhelmed.

Another reason small steps lead to big changes lies in their ability to foster habits. Habits are the foundation of long-term success, as they automate behaviors and reduce the need for constant willpower. Starting with small, manageable actions makes it easier to establish new habits. For example, committing to five minutes of meditation each morning is far more achievable than attempting an hour-long practice right away. Once the smaller habit becomes ingrained, it can be expanded gradually. This process, often referred to as "habit stacking," allows you to build complex routines by layering new habits onto existing ones. Over time, these micro-routines solidify, creating a framework for sustained success.

Small steps are particularly effective in overcoming fear and resistance. Large goals often trigger feelings of self-doubt or fear of failure, which can paralyze action. However, taking a single, low-stakes step reduces the psychological weight of starting. It's easier to write one sentence than to commit to completing an entire novel. It's less intimidating to take a short walk than to plan a marathon training regimen. By focusing on what feels achievable in the moment, you build courage and diminish the fear that holds you back. Each small victory reinforces your belief in your ability to succeed, creating a positive feedback loop.

The concept of "minimum viable action" further illustrates the power of small steps. This approach involves identifying the smallest possible action you can take toward your goal and committing to it. For example, if your goal is to improve your fitness, your minimum viable action might be putting on your workout clothes. This tiny step often leads to the next—stretching, walking, or completing a short workout. By starting small, you eliminate excuses and create a sense of accomplishment, which propels you forward. The simplicity of this approach makes it accessible to anyone, regardless of circumstances or resources.

Small steps also allow for flexibility and adaptability. Life is unpredictable, and rigid plans often falter in the face of unexpected challenges. By focusing on incremental progress, you can adjust your actions without losing sight of your goals. For instance, if a busy schedule prevents you from completing an hour-long study session, dedicating just ten minutes to review material ensures continued progress. This adaptability prevents setbacks from derailing your efforts and keeps you moving forward, even when circumstances are less than ideal.

The science of neuroplasticity supports the effectiveness of small steps. The brain has an incredible capacity to adapt and rewire itself in response to new experiences. Repeated actions, even small ones, strengthen neural pathways associated with those behaviors. Over time, this rewiring makes the actions easier and more automatic. For example, consistently practicing a musical instrument for a few minutes each day gradually improves skill and confidence. The same principle applies to any area of growth—whether learning a new language, developing a skill, or adopting healthier habits. Small, consistent actions create lasting change at the neurological level.

Celebrating small wins is another essential aspect of this approach. Acknowledging and rewarding your progress reinforces positive behavior and boosts motivation. Whether it's treating yourself to a favorite snack after completing a task or simply taking a moment to reflect on your achievements, these celebrations create a sense of joy and satisfaction. This emotional reinforcement strengthens your commitment to the process and makes the journey toward your goals more enjoyable. Success becomes not just an end result but an ongoing experience, marked by moments of pride and fulfillment.

Small steps also teach patience and persistence. In a culture that often glorifies instant results, the slow, steady approach can feel counterintuitive. However, true change requires time and effort. By embracing the process and focusing on consistent progress, you develop resilience and a deeper appreciation for the journey. This mindset shift transforms setbacks into learning opportunities and fosters a sense of gratitude for each step forward. The ability to persevere through challenges, however minor, builds character and prepares you for greater achievements.

Exploring the Neuroscience of Consistency

Consistency is the thread that weaves together actions, habits, and progress into meaningful, lasting change. Understanding the neuroscience behind consistency offers a fascinating glimpse into how the brain works to support—or hinder—our efforts to achieve goals. The principles that govern consistency are deeply embedded in the biological and chemical processes of the brain, and by leveraging this knowledge, one can create an environment where consistent behavior becomes second nature. Far from being just a matter of willpower, consistency is tied to the way the brain processes rewards, forms connections, and adapts to repeated actions over time.

The brain craves predictability and thrives on patterns. At its core, the brain is an organ of efficiency—it seeks to conserve energy by automating repetitive behaviors through a process called myelination. Myelin is a fatty substance that coats neural pathways, making communication between neurons faster and more efficient. When you perform an action repeatedly, the neural pathways associated with that behavior become myelinated, effectively making the action easier to perform and more automatic. This is why behaviors practiced consistently, whether positive or negative, become habits over time. The brain rewards repeated patterns by reducing the effort required to execute them, encouraging their continuation.

Consistency also taps into the brain's reward system, which is governed by the neurotransmitter dopamine. Dopamine is often associated with pleasure, but its primary role is to reinforce behaviors that lead to rewards. When you perform a task and achieve a satisfying outcome, your brain releases dopamine, creating a sense of accomplishment and signaling that the behavior is worth repeating. Over time, the act of simply engaging in the behavior can trigger a dopamine release, even before a tangible reward is achieved. For example, a consistent morning run may eventually provide a sense of satisfaction and motivation on its own, without the need for an external reward like weight loss or improved fitness. This is the brain's way of encouraging consistency by making the process itself enjoyable.

The concept of neuroplasticity further underscores the importance of consistency in shaping behavior. Neuroplasticity refers to the brain's ability to rewire itself in response to experiences and repeated actions. Each time you engage in a behavior, you strengthen the neural pathways associated with it, making it more likely that you will repeat the behavior in the future. This is why consistency is so critical—sporadic efforts fail to create the lasting neural changes needed to support long-term habits and goals. The brain requires repeated exposure to a behavior to recognize it as a priority and allocate resources to solidify it into your daily routine.

The prefrontal cortex, the brain region responsible for decision-making, self-control, and planning, plays a pivotal role in maintaining consistency. This area of the brain acts as a regulator, helping you weigh long-term benefits against short-term impulses. However, the prefrontal cortex has its limitations—it is prone to fatigue and can only handle a finite number of decisions and self-control tasks in a given period. This is where the power of routine and automation comes into play. By creating consistent routines, you reduce the cognitive load on your prefrontal cortex, freeing up mental energy for more complex decisions and challenges.

Stress and inconsistency often go hand in hand, and the role of the amygdala—a part of the brain involved in processing emotions—cannot be overlooked. When you experience stress, the amygdala becomes hyperactive, impairing the functioning of the prefrontal cortex and making it harder to stick to consistent behaviors. This is why stressful situations often lead to lapses in routines, such as skipping workouts, overeating, or procrastinating. Managing stress through techniques like mindfulness, meditation, or physical activity can help regulate the amygdala and support consistent behavior even in challenging circumstances.

The brain's relationship with consistency is also influenced by the concept of time. The basal ganglia, a region of the brain involved in habit formation, relies on regularity to embed behaviors into your subconscious. Actions performed at the same time each day are more likely to become automatic because the brain begins to associate specific cues—such as the time of day or a particular environment—with the behavior. For instance, consistently going to bed at the same time every night helps regulate your circadian rhythm, leading to better sleep quality. Similarly, scheduling daily study sessions at the same hour trains your brain to focus and prepare for the task at hand. Time-based triggers act as cues for consistent behaviors, reinforcing the neural pathways associated with those actions.

The power of consistency is further amplified by the brain's tendency to seek closure and completion. The Zeigarnik effect, a psychological phenomenon, suggests that unfinished tasks linger in the mind, creating a sense of mental discomfort. Completing tasks consistently provides a sense of resolution and satisfaction, which the brain finds rewarding. This is why breaking larger goals into smaller, manageable tasks and completing them regularly can create a snowball effect of motivation and productivity. Each completed task reinforces the behavior, making it easier to maintain consistency over time.

While the brain supports consistency in many ways, it also presents challenges that must be navigated to sustain it. One such challenge is the brain's natural inclination toward novelty and instant gratification. The limbic system, often referred to as the brain's emotional center, is driven by a desire for immediate rewards and stimulation. This can make it difficult to stick to consistent behaviors, especially when the rewards are delayed or intangible. Overcoming this challenge requires a deliberate effort to focus on the long-term benefits of consistency and to find ways to make the process itself engaging and rewarding.

Another obstacle is the brain's tendency to revert to default behaviors under conditions of fatigue or stress. When the prefrontal cortex is depleted, the brain relies on established habits and routines to navigate the day. If these default behaviors are inconsistent or counterproductive, they can undermine progress toward your goals. This is why building consistency requires not only repetition but also a focus on creating positive default behaviors that align with your long-term objectives. By embedding these behaviors into your subconscious through consistent practice, you create a safety net that supports your goals even when willpower is low.

Consistency also requires patience, as the brain's processes of adapting and rewiring take time. The immediate results that many people crave are often at odds with the gradual nature of neural change. Understanding that consistency is a long-term investment helps to manage expectations and maintain motivation. Celebrating small milestones along the way provides the brain with the reinforcement it needs to stay committed to the process.

The interplay between consistency and identity offers another layer of insight. The brain aligns behaviors with self-perception, meaning that consistent actions reinforce your sense of identity, and vice versa. If you consistently act in ways that reflect discipline, focus, and commitment, your brain begins to internalize these traits as part of your identity. This creates a feedback loop where your actions and identity reinforce one another, making it easier to sustain consistent behaviors over time.

To leverage the neuroscience of consistency, it is essential to create an environment and structure that supports repeated actions. This includes minimizing distractions, establishing clear routines, and setting specific, achievable goals. By aligning your environment with your intentions, you reduce the mental friction that often derails consistency. Additionally, surrounding yourself with supportive individuals who reinforce consistent behavior can have a profound impact. Social influences play a significant role in shaping behavior, and being part of a community that values consistency can provide the accountability and encouragement needed to stay on track.

Chapter 3: Breaking Barriers Confronting Resistance

Overcoming Procrastination and Fear

Procrastination and fear form a complex partnership, silently undermining ambitions and keeping people trapped in cycles of hesitation. They don't announce themselves loudly but manifest subtly, often masquerading as harmless delays or rational justifications. Yet, their impact is potent, weaving barriers between aspirations and actions. To overcome them, one must first understand how they operate, their psychological roots, and the practical methods to dismantle their influence step by step.

Procrastination often arises from an emotional root rather than a purely logical one. It's rarely about time management, as many assume; instead, it frequently stems from avoiding discomfort. This discomfort might come in the form of fear—fear of failure, fear of judgment, or even fear of success. For instance, a person might delay starting a project not because they lack the time but because they're overwhelmed by the potential of not meeting expectations. The task grows larger in their mind with every passing day, and avoidance becomes a temporary refuge. However, this refuge is deceptive. While procrastination may offer short-term relief, it compounds stress and anxiety over the long term, leaving the individual feeling stuck in a state of inaction.

Fear, on the other hand, thrives on uncertainty. It magnifies risks and distorts reality, transforming manageable challenges into seemingly insurmountable obstacles. The fear of failure, for example, often convinces people that taking no action is better than risking an imperfect result. This mindset is paralyzing. A writer, for example, may avoid starting a novel because they're haunted by thoughts of rejection or criticism. The blank page becomes a mirror reflecting their doubts, and so they procrastinate, convincing themselves they'll begin "when inspiration strikes" or "when the timing is better." But fear and procrastination are skilled collaborators—they create a self-perpetuating cycle that thrives on delay and hesitation.

Breaking free from this cycle begins with awareness. Recognizing procrastination as a behavior rooted in avoidance rather than laziness is a crucial first step. The next is understanding the specific fears driving that avoidance. Naming these fears diminishes their power. For example, acknowledging that you're afraid of public speaking because you fear embarrassment allows you to address the emotion rather than letting it fester unchecked. Awareness transforms abstract fears into tangible challenges that can be confronted.

Once fears are identified, reframing them becomes essential. Fear often tricks the mind into believing that failure is catastrophic when, in reality, it's a natural and necessary part of growth. People frequently recall stories of successful individuals who failed multiple times before achieving their goals. Thomas Edison famously failed thousands of times before inventing the lightbulb, yet he reframed each failure as a step closer to success. This perspective doesn't erase fear but puts it into context, making it less paralyzing. Instead of viewing failure as an endpoint, it can be seen as data, feedback, and part of the process.

Action is the antidote to procrastination and fear. Even the smallest step forward can disrupt their grip. Momentum is a powerful force; taking a single action, no matter how small, creates a ripple effect that makes subsequent actions easier. For example, if writing an entire essay feels overwhelming, committing to writing just the first sentence can lower the barrier to entry. Once the first sentence is on the page, the task no longer feels as daunting. The brain rewards action with a sense of accomplishment, releasing dopamine, the "feel-good" neurotransmitter. This reward reinforces the behavior, making it easier to continue.

Breaking tasks into smaller, more manageable pieces is another effective strategy. Fear often amplifies when a goal feels too large or undefined. Writing a book, for instance, might feel overwhelming as a whole, but writing one paragraph a day feels achievable. These small, consistent actions build confidence and reduce the mental resistance that fuels procrastination. Moreover, completing smaller tasks provides a sense of progress, counteracting the stagnation that fear and procrastination create. Each completed step becomes evidence that the larger goal is within reach, chipping away at doubts along the way.

The environment also plays a significant role in procrastination. A cluttered or distracting space can amplify avoidance behaviors. Creating an environment that encourages focus and minimizes distractions can significantly enhance productivity. For example, turning off notifications, organizing a workspace, or setting specific times for focused work can reduce opportunities for procrastination. The brain thrives on cues and routines, so associating a particular space or time with a specific task can reinforce consistent action. Over time, this association becomes automatic, further reducing the effort needed to begin.

Time management techniques, like the Pomodoro Technique, are valuable tools for overcoming procrastination. By working in short, focused intervals—typically 25 minutes—followed by brief breaks, tasks become less intimidating and more approachable. This method capitalizes on the brain's natural attention span, preventing burnout and maintaining engagement. Setting clear, achievable goals for each interval provides structure and a sense of accomplishment, which motivates further progress. Additionally, tracking completed intervals serves as a visual reminder of productivity, counteracting the self-doubt that procrastination often fosters.

Accountability can also disrupt the cycles of fear and procrastination. Sharing goals with a trusted friend, mentor, or group creates a sense of responsibility that encourages follow-through. Knowing that someone else is aware of your commitments adds an external layer of motivation. This accountability doesn't have to be formal; even a simple check-in with a friend can provide the encouragement needed to take the next step. For those who prefer solitude, journaling about progress can serve a similar purpose, offering a space to reflect on achievements and identify patterns of avoidance.

Self-compassion is often overlooked but essential in combating procrastination and fear. People who procrastinate frequently criticize themselves, creating a cycle of guilt and shame that perpetuates inaction. Treating yourself with kindness and understanding breaks this cycle. Acknowledge that struggling with procrastination is a common human experience and that it doesn't define your worth or potential. Celebrate small victories, no matter how minor they may seem, and remind yourself that progress, not perfection, is the goal.

Visualization is another powerful tool for overcoming fear. The mind is deeply influenced by imagery, and imagining yourself successfully completing a task can create a sense of familiarity and reduce anxiety. For example, if the thought of delivering a presentation fills you with dread, close your eyes and picture yourself speaking confidently, receiving positive feedback, and feeling proud of your effort. This mental rehearsal primes the brain for success and reinforces the belief that you're capable of handling challenges.

Finally, it's important to challenge the myths and assumptions that procrastination and fear perpetuate. These emotions often convince you that waiting for the "perfect moment" is necessary, but the truth is, perfection is an illusion. Waiting for ideal conditions is another form of avoidance, one that keeps you in limbo. Progress doesn't require perfection; it requires action. Embracing imperfection allows you to move forward, learn, and adapt along the way.

Identifying and Conquering Limiting Beliefs

Limiting beliefs are the invisible chains that restrict potential, holding individuals back from achieving what they are truly capable of. They often operate beneath the surface of conscious thought, shaping perceptions, decisions, and behaviors in ways that reinforce self-imposed boundaries. These beliefs are not facts, yet they feel deeply rooted and unshakable, often stemming from past experiences, societal conditioning, or narratives absorbed during formative years. The process of identifying and conquering limiting beliefs is a transformative journey, one that requires introspection, courage, and deliberate action to rewrite the stories that define personal possibilities.

At their core, limiting beliefs are assumptions or convictions about oneself, others, or the world that constrain choices and actions. They manifest in statements like, "I'm not smart enough," "I don't deserve success," or "I'll never be good at this." These beliefs may seem trivial at first glance, but their influence is profound, shaping how individuals approach challenges, opportunities, and relationships. For example, someone who believes they are "bad at math" might avoid careers or projects that require analytical thinking, even if they possess untapped potential in those areas. Over time, the avoidance reinforces the belief, creating a self-fulfilling prophecy that cements the limitation.

The origins of limiting beliefs are as varied as the individuals who hold them. Many are rooted in childhood experiences, where comments from authority figures—parents, teachers, or peers—leave lasting impressions. A child repeatedly told they are "too shy" may internalize this label, perceiving themselves as socially inept well into adulthood. Similarly, societal messages about success, beauty, or intelligence can contribute to beliefs that dictate what is "possible" or "acceptable." Failures, disappointments, or traumatic events also play a role, as the mind seeks to rationalize these experiences by attributing them to personal inadequacies or inherent flaws. While these beliefs may have served a protective purpose at one time, shielding individuals from perceived risks or rejection, they eventually outlive their usefulness and become obstacles to growth.

Identifying limiting beliefs requires a willingness to confront the stories you tell yourself. Start by examining areas of life where you feel stuck, unfulfilled, or consistently frustrated. These patterns often point to underlying beliefs that are shaping your reality. For instance, if you find yourself avoiding leadership opportunities despite a desire to advance in your career, ask yourself why. What thoughts arise at the prospect of taking on such a role? Do you believe you lack the skills, that others are more qualified, or that you'll inevitably fail? These questions reveal the internal scripts running in the background, scripts that need to be brought to light.

Journaling is a powerful tool for uncovering limiting beliefs. Setting aside time to write about your fears, doubts, and recurring thoughts allows you to observe patterns and themes without judgment. Pay attention to phrases that begin with "I can't," "I'm not," or "I'll never," as these often signal underlying beliefs. For example, writing, "I can't start my own business because I'm not an expert," reveals a belief that expertise is a prerequisite for success—a belief worth challenging. The act of putting these thoughts on paper externalizes them, making it easier to analyze their validity and origin.

Once identified, the next step is to question the truth of these beliefs. Limiting beliefs often go unchallenged because they feel so ingrained, but that doesn't make them factual. Ask yourself, "Is this belief objectively true? What evidence supports it, and what evidence contradicts it?" For example, if you believe you're "not creative," consider instances where you've solved problems, come up with ideas, or approached situations in unique ways. These examples challenge the narrative, planting seeds of doubt in the belief's validity. Additionally, consider the source of the belief. If it originated from someone else's opinion or an isolated experience, recognize that it may not reflect your true capabilities or potential.

Reframing is a vital part of conquering limiting beliefs. This involves replacing disempowering thoughts with empowering ones that align with your goals and values. For instance, instead of thinking, "I'm not experienced enough to apply for this job," reframe it to, "Everyone starts somewhere, and I can learn and grow in this role." Reframing doesn't mean ignoring challenges or pretending limitations don't exist; rather, it shifts the focus from obstacles to possibilities. Over time, consistent reframing rewires thought patterns, transforming limiting beliefs into empowering ones.

Taking action is a crucial step in dismantling limiting beliefs. Beliefs are reinforced through inaction, as avoidance validates their hold. To break free, it's essential to confront fears and doubts head-on, even in small ways. If you believe you're "not good at public speaking," for example, start by speaking up in a small meeting or practicing a presentation in front of a trusted friend. Each action, no matter how minor, challenges the belief and builds evidence that contradicts it. Over time, these actions create a new narrative—one of capability and resilience.

Surrounding yourself with supportive influences can also accelerate the process of conquering limiting beliefs. The people you spend time with shape your mindset, either reinforcing limitations or encouraging growth. Seek out individuals who inspire and uplift you, who challenge you to see beyond perceived boundaries. Their perspectives and encouragement can help you reframe beliefs and expand your sense of what's possible. Additionally, consuming stories, books, or media that highlight resilience and achievement can provide powerful counterexamples to limiting narratives.

It's important to acknowledge that overcoming limiting beliefs is not a one-time event but an ongoing process. These beliefs often resurface, especially in new or challenging situations. When they do, return to the tools that helped you identify and challenge them in the first place. Practice self-compassion, recognizing that growth is a journey with ups and downs. Celebrate progress, no matter how small, as each step forward weakens the hold of limiting beliefs and strengthens your capacity for change.

The relationship between beliefs and reality is reciprocal. Limiting beliefs shape actions, which in turn shape outcomes, reinforcing the beliefs. But the reverse is also true: changing beliefs changes actions, which changes outcomes, creating a positive feedback loop. Consider someone who believes they are "not athletic." This belief might lead them to avoid exercise, reinforcing a sedentary lifestyle that validates the belief. However, if they challenge this narrative by starting a gentle fitness routine and gradually building strength and confidence, their actions create new evidence that contradicts the original belief. Over time, the narrative shifts from "I'm not athletic" to "I'm improving my fitness every day."

The power of identity cannot be overstated in conquering limiting beliefs. People act in alignment with who they believe they are. Shifting beliefs about identity—how you see yourself—creates lasting change. Instead of focusing solely on outcomes, focus on becoming the type of person who embodies the values and behaviors you aspire to. For example, rather than setting a goal to "run a marathon," adopt the identity of "I am a runner." This identity shift aligns your actions with your beliefs, making consistency and growth feel natural rather than forced.

Leveraging the Power of Emotional Resilience

Emotional resilience is the ability to adapt to stress, adversity, and challenges with a sense of equilibrium and strength. It is not about avoiding hardship but rather navigating through it with a mindset that allows growth instead of defeat. Life is filled with unpredictability, and emotional resilience acts as a stabilizing force, helping individuals maintain clarity, focus, and purpose despite the turbulence. Those who cultivate this skill not only recover from setbacks more effectively but also build the capacity to thrive in situations that would otherwise overwhelm them.

Resilience begins with self-awareness. Understanding your emotional responses during tough situations provides a foundation for managing them. For instance, when faced with rejection, do you tend to spiral into self-doubt, or are you able to reflect on the experience with perspective? Recognizing these patterns is a crucial step in building resilience. Emotional reactions are often automatic, shaped by past experiences and deeply ingrained beliefs. By observing them without judgment, you create space to respond intentionally rather than react impulsively.

A key characteristic of emotional resilience is the ability to regulate emotions. This doesn't mean suppressing feelings but understanding them and responding in a way that aligns with your values and goals. Imagine receiving critical feedback at work. An unregulated response might involve defensiveness or anger, which can escalate the situation and damage relationships. A resilient response, however, would involve pausing to process the feedback, separating its constructive elements from any emotional sting, and using it as an opportunity for growth. Emotional regulation transforms challenges into stepping stones rather than stumbling blocks.

Perspective plays a significant role in emotional resilience. When faced with adversity, it is easy to catastrophize, imagining worst-case scenarios that heighten stress and anxiety. Resilient individuals, however, practice reframing—viewing challenges through a lens of opportunity or learning. For example, losing a job might initially feel devastating, but with a resilient perspective, it can be reframed as a chance to explore new career paths or develop new skills. This shift in mindset doesn't diminish the difficulty of the situation but allows for a more constructive response, opening the door to possibilities that might otherwise be overlooked.

Building resilience also involves cultivating a strong sense of self-efficacy—the belief in your ability to influence events and outcomes. People with high self-efficacy approach challenges with confidence, seeing them as problems to solve rather than threats to avoid. This belief is not innate but developed through experience. Tackling small challenges and celebrating successes along the way reinforces the sense that you are capable of handling difficulties. Each victory, no matter how small, builds the foundation for facing larger obstacles with assurance.

Social connections are another cornerstone of emotional resilience. Humans are inherently social beings, and the support of trusted individuals can make a profound difference during times of hardship. Resilient people understand the value of reaching out, whether for advice, encouragement, or simply to share their experiences. This doesn't mean relying on others to solve your problems but recognizing that vulnerability and connection are strengths, not weaknesses. A strong support network acts as a safety net, providing perspective and reassurance when your own resilience feels stretched thin.

Another critical aspect of building emotional resilience is embracing adaptability. Rigidity in the face of change often leads to frustration and resistance, while flexibility opens the door to solutions and opportunities. Life rarely unfolds exactly as planned, and the ability to pivot when circumstances shift is a hallmark of resilience. Consider an athlete who sustains an injury that derails their training. A rigid mindset might dwell on the setback, seeing it as a failure or an insurmountable obstacle. An adaptable mindset, however, would focus on rehabilitation, exploring alternative workouts, or even discovering new interests. Adaptability doesn't eliminate challenges but equips you to navigate them with creativity and resourcefulness.

Resilient individuals also understand the importance of maintaining physical and mental well-being. Stress and adversity take a toll on the body and mind, and neglecting self-care during tough times can exacerbate the impact. Prioritizing sleep, nutrition, and exercise creates a foundation of strength that supports emotional resilience. Similarly, practices like mindfulness and meditation help manage stress, providing tools to stay present and grounded even in the midst of chaos. These habits are not luxuries but necessities, forming a buffer against the wear and tear of life's challenges.

A sense of purpose is another element that strengthens emotional resilience. Having a clear understanding of your values and goals provides a compass that guides you through adversity. When setbacks occur, purpose acts as an anchor, reminding you why persistence matters. For example, a parent working multiple jobs to support their family may draw strength from their commitment to providing a better future for their children. Purpose doesn't eliminate difficulties but imbues them with meaning, making it easier to endure and overcome them.

Practicing gratitude can also fortify resilience. During tough times, it is easy to focus solely on what's going wrong, which magnifies negativity and diminishes hope. Gratitude shifts attention to what is still good and positive, providing a counterbalance to adversity. This doesn't mean ignoring challenges but acknowledging the aspects of life that bring joy or comfort, however small they may be. For instance, even in the midst of a difficult period, taking a moment to appreciate supportive friends, a beautiful sunset, or a personal achievement can provide a boost of perspective and optimism.

Failures and setbacks are inevitable, but resilient individuals view them as opportunities for growth rather than evidence of inadequacy. This mindset, often referred to as a "growth mindset," sees challenges as a chance to develop skills, gain insights, and build character. For example, a student who performs poorly on an exam might use the experience to identify weaknesses and improve study habits rather than concluding that they are inherently bad at the subject. This approach encourages persistence and effort, turning obstacles into catalysts for improvement.

Resilience also involves accepting what cannot be changed. Some challenges are beyond control, and fighting against them only drains energy and increases frustration. Acceptance doesn't mean giving up but acknowledging reality and focusing on what can be influenced. For example, after a natural disaster, survivors cannot undo the event but can focus on rebuilding and supporting their communities. This shift from resistance to proactive engagement creates a sense of empowerment even in the face of uncontrollable circumstances.

Cultivating emotional resilience is not a one-time effort but an ongoing practice. Life will continually present new challenges, each testing your capacity to adapt and persevere. The strategies that build resilience—self-awareness, emotional regulation, perspective, self-efficacy, social connections, adaptability, well-being, purpose, gratitude, a growth mindset, and acceptance—are not static tools but dynamic skills that evolve with experience. Each encounter with adversity provides an opportunity to strengthen these skills, deepening your reservoir of resilience for the future.

Chapter 4: Designing Your Discipline Framework

Building Your Personal System of Success

A personal system of success is the architecture that supports consistent progress and achievement. It is not built on fleeting motivation or random efforts but on deliberate habits, routines, and strategies that align with your goals and values. The concept of success can be deeply personal, varying from one individual to another. For some, it might mean career advancement, while for others, it could signify personal growth, fulfilling relationships, or maintaining a balanced lifestyle. Regardless of the definition, a well-designed system is what transforms aspirations into reality.

The foundation of any effective personal system begins with clarity of purpose. Without a clear sense of direction, even the most disciplined efforts can feel aimless or misaligned. Start by identifying what success means to you, not what society, culture, or others dictate. This step requires introspection and honesty. What drives you? What legacy do you want to leave behind? What goals truly excite you? These questions help uncover your core motivations. A person pursuing financial independence, for example, might realize their motivation stems not from a desire for wealth but from the freedom it provides to spend time with loved ones or pursue creative passions.

With this clarity, you can build a system tailored to your unique aspirations.

Once your purpose is defined, breaking it down into actionable goals is the next step. Lofty ambitions, while inspiring, can be overwhelming without a roadmap. A system thrives on structure, so take the time to translate long-term aspirations into smaller, manageable milestones. For instance, if your goal is to write a novel, break it into specific tasks: outlining the story, developing characters, setting a daily word count, and scheduling time for editing. These actionable steps create a sense of progress, preventing the paralysis that often accompanies large, undefined objectives. Success becomes less about achieving one monumental milestone and more about consistently moving forward, one step at a time.

Habits form the backbone of a personal system of success. While willpower and motivation can spark action, they are fleeting and unreliable over the long term. Habits, on the other hand, automate behavior, reducing the mental energy required to make decisions. To build effective habits, focus on consistency over intensity. A person aiming to get in shape, for example, might start with a ten-minute walk each day rather than committing to an hour-long workout they are unlikely to sustain. Over time, this small habit can be expanded and built upon, creating a routine that feels natural rather than forced.

The environment in which you operate plays a critical role in reinforcing your system. A well-designed environment minimizes friction and makes it easier to stay on track. Consider how your surroundings can either support or hinder your progress. If your goal is to eat healthier, stocking your kitchen with nutritious options and removing junk food eliminates unnecessary temptations. Similarly, organizing your workspace to reduce distractions can enhance focus and productivity. These environmental adjustments may seem minor, but they have a cumulative effect, making it easier to follow through on your intentions.

Time management is another essential component. A successful system prioritizes what matters most and allocates time accordingly. Begin by identifying your most important tasks—the ones that directly contribute to your goals—and schedule them during your peak energy hours. For some, this might mean tackling creative projects in the morning when their mind is fresh, while others may find their productivity peaks in the evening. Avoid filling your schedule with busywork that feels productive but doesn't move the needle. Instead, focus on high-impact activities that align with your purpose. Tools like time blocking, where specific hours are set aside for focused work, can be particularly effective in maintaining discipline and avoiding distractions.

Feedback and reflection are crucial for refining your system. No plan is perfect from the outset, and adjustments are inevitable as you learn what works and what doesn't. Set aside regular intervals to evaluate your progress. Are you meeting your milestones? Are your habits sustainable? What obstacles are consistently derailing you? For example, someone pursuing a fitness goal might discover that evening workouts are frequently skipped due to exhaustion after work. By reflecting on this pattern, they could adjust their schedule to prioritize morning workouts instead. This iterative process ensures your system evolves alongside your needs and circumstances.

Resilience is another key element. Even the most well-constructed system will face setbacks—unexpected challenges, failures, or moments of doubt. Building resilience into your system involves anticipating obstacles and preparing strategies to overcome them. For example, if procrastination is a recurring issue, creating accountability mechanisms, such as sharing your goals with a trusted friend or mentor, can help keep you on track. Similarly, having contingency plans for unavoidable disruptions ensures that a single setback doesn't derail your entire system. A missed workout or an unproductive day doesn't have to spiral into a week or month of inactivity. Resilient systems are built to bend, not break.

Celebrating progress is just as important as achieving results. Acknowledging small wins along the way reinforces positive behavior and keeps motivation high. These celebrations don't have to be extravagant—a simple acknowledgment of your efforts or a reward tied to a milestone can be enough. For instance, completing the first draft of a project might be an opportunity to treat yourself to a favorite meal or take a day off to recharge. Celebrating progress reminds you that success is a journey, not just a destination, and helps sustain momentum over the long term.

Another often-overlooked aspect of a successful system is the role of energy management. Success is not solely about time and effort but also about maintaining the physical, mental, and emotional energy required to perform at your best. Prioritize sleep, nutrition, and exercise to keep your body and mind in optimal condition. Equally important is managing stress and fostering a positive mindset. Practices like mindfulness, gratitude, or hobbies that bring joy can replenish energy and prevent burnout. A well-rounded system considers not only what you need to do but also how you need to feel to sustain peak performance.

Surrounding yourself with the right people can amplify the effectiveness of your system. Supportive relationships provide encouragement, accountability, and inspiration, while toxic or unsupportive influences can drain energy and derail progress. Seek out mentors, peers, or communities that share your values and goals. Their insights and experiences can provide valuable perspectives, and their belief in your potential can bolster your confidence during moments of doubt. Conversely, learning to set boundaries with those who undermine your efforts is equally important. Your system thrives when it is reinforced by a network of relationships aligned with your vision.

Flexibility is the final piece of the puzzle. Life is unpredictable, and rigid systems are prone to collapse under the weight of unforeseen circumstances. A flexible system adapts to changing priorities, unexpected challenges, or new opportunities. For example, a person juggling work and family responsibilities might need to adjust their routines during particularly busy periods. Flexibility doesn't mean abandoning structure; it means designing your system to accommodate change without losing sight of your goals. This adaptability ensures your system remains effective over time, regardless of the circumstances.

Aligning Goals with Core Values

Goals are often seen as the markers of progress, the milestones that signify achievement. Yet, goals without alignment to core values can lead to a hollow sense of accomplishment. They may propel you to a destination that, upon arrival, feels foreign or unfulfilling. Core values act as a compass, grounding your ambitions in principles that resonate deeply with who you are. When goals and values are in harmony, every step forward feels purposeful, and success becomes more than just an external win—it becomes an internal affirmation of your identity.

Core values are the fundamental beliefs that shape your choices, preferences, and sense of right and wrong. They are not fleeting desires or momentary interests but enduring principles that guide your actions and priorities. For instance, someone who values family deeply may prioritize time with loved ones over career ambitions, while another who values creativity might seek opportunities to express their originality, even at the expense of financial stability. Identifying these values requires introspection, as they are often buried beneath societal expectations, cultural norms, or the influence of others. To uncover your core values, consider the moments in your life that have felt most meaningful and fulfilling. What principles were at play? What made those experiences resonate so strongly with you?

Imagine a person who values independence but sets a goal to climb the corporate ladder in a traditional organization. On the surface, this goal might appear ambitious and respectable, but over time, the rigid structure of the environment may feel stifling, leading to dissatisfaction despite outward success. This disconnect occurs because the goal conflicts with the individual's core value of independence. Alignment, on the other hand, would involve pursuing entrepreneurial ventures or roles that allow for autonomy, ensuring that the journey and destination both honor their fundamental beliefs.

The process of aligning goals with core values begins with clarity. Without a deep understanding of what truly matters to you, it is easy to adopt goals that reflect external pressures rather than internal desires. Start by reflecting on what you stand for. What principles are non-negotiable in your life? What legacy do you wish to leave behind? These questions help articulate the foundation upon which your goals should be built. For example, if one of your core values is integrity, any goal that requires compromising your honesty or principles will ultimately feel misaligned, no matter how lucrative or prestigious it may be.

It's equally important to recognize when your goals are being shaped by external influences rather than your internal compass. Societal expectations, cultural norms, and the opinions of those around you often exert a powerful pull, steering you toward objectives that may not reflect your authentic self. A person raised in a family that values financial success above all else might feel pressured to pursue a high-paying career, even if their true passion lies in the arts or public service. While the external validation that comes with meeting these expectations can be gratifying in the short term, it often leads to frustration or burnout as the disconnect between values and goals becomes apparent.

To align your goals with your core values, begin by conducting an audit of your current objectives. Write down your goals and then evaluate each one against your values. Ask yourself, "Does this goal reflect what truly matters to me? Will achieving it bring me closer to the life I want to lead, or is it simply a stepping stone toward someone else's vision of success?" This process often reveals goals that feel out of sync, as well as those that align perfectly. For example, a goal to work longer hours to earn a promotion might clash with a value of prioritizing health or family time, while a goal to build a supportive community at work may align beautifully with values of connection and teamwork.

When misalignment is identified, it's essential to recalibrate rather than discard. A goal that feels out of sync with your values can often be adjusted to better reflect your principles. Consider the example of someone who values adventure and sets a goal to travel the world but finds themselves stuck in a job that limits their ability to explore. Instead of abandoning their job altogether, they might recalibrate by seeking remote work opportunities or scheduling periodic sabbaticals, allowing them to honor their value of adventure while maintaining their career. This process of adjustment ensures that aspirations remain both achievable and meaningful.

Another critical aspect of alignment is ensuring that the journey toward your goals reflects your values, not just the destination. It's easy to justify compromising values in the pursuit of a long-term objective, telling yourself that the ends will justify the means. However, this approach often leads to dissonance and regret. Consider the case of a business owner who values sustainability but cuts corners on environmentally friendly practices to maximize profit. While they may achieve financial success in the short term, the misalignment between their actions and values may lead to a sense of unease or dissatisfaction. Instead, staying true to sustainability throughout the journey ensures that success feels authentic and rewarding.

A powerful tool for maintaining alignment is visualization. Picture yourself achieving a goal and then reflect on how it feels. Does it evoke a sense of pride, fulfillment, or joy? Or does it feel hollow, as though something essential is missing? Visualization helps you test the emotional resonance of a goal before committing to it, ensuring that it aligns with your values. For example, someone considering a high-powered career move might visualize the long hours, stress, and impact on personal relationships that come with it. If the image feels at odds with their values of balance and connection, it may prompt a reevaluation of priorities.

Accountability also plays a significant role in staying aligned. Share your goals and values with trusted friends, mentors, or family members who understand your principles and can provide honest feedback. These individuals can help you identify when you're veering off course and encourage you to stay true to your values. For instance, a friend who knows you value creativity might gently remind you to prioritize your art when you become consumed by the demands of a less fulfilling job. This external perspective can provide clarity and reinforcement, helping you navigate the complexities of balancing goals and values.

It's important to acknowledge that values and priorities can evolve over time. What resonates deeply with you at one stage of life may shift as circumstances, experiences, and perspectives change. Periodic reflection ensures that your goals remain aligned with your current values, rather than being anchored to outdated or irrelevant principles. For example, a person who values adventure in their youth might find that stability and security become more important as they start a family. This evolution is natural and should be embraced rather than resisted, allowing your goals to grow and adapt alongside you.

The alignment of goals and values creates a sense of congruence that enhances motivation, resilience, and satisfaction. When you pursue objectives that reflect your principles, every step forward feels purposeful, and challenges become more manageable because they are in service of something meaningful. Success is no longer just about reaching a destination; it's about the integrity of the journey and the fulfillment that comes from living in accordance with your values.

Chapter 5: Morning Mastery Setting the Tone for Success

Crafting a Powerful Morning Routine

Mornings set the tone for the rest of the day. They hold a unique potential—a quiet pocket of time unmarred by the chaos of commitments and distractions that inevitably build as the hours progress. A powerful morning routine is not merely a collection of tasks to check off; it is a deliberate, personal sequence designed to sharpen focus, boost energy, and align your mindset with your goals. It's about creating a foundation that makes the rest of the day more effective, intentional, and fulfilling.

The first step in crafting a morning routine that works for you is understanding its purpose. It isn't about mimicking someone else's ideal morning or adhering to rigid, overly ambitious schedules. Instead, it's about designing a routine that reflects your priorities and sets the stage for the kind of day you want to have. For example, an entrepreneur might use their morning to strategize and reflect, while a parent may prioritize moments of calm before attending to their family's needs. A powerful routine is personal, built around what fuels you mentally, physically, and emotionally.

Waking up intentionally is the cornerstone of any strong morning routine. The way you transition from sleep to wakefulness can dictate your mood and productivity for the hours to come. Instead of jolting awake to an alarm and immediately diving into emails or social media, consider a gentler start. Begin with a few moments of stillness to orient yourself, whether that's through deep breathing, stretching, or simply sitting quietly. This small habit creates a buffer, giving you control over your morning before external demands take over. It transforms waking up from a rushed, reactive process into a deliberate practice.

Hydration is another simple yet transformative habit. After hours of sleep, your body craves water to replenish and kickstart metabolic processes. Reaching for a glass of water first thing not only aids physical health but also signals to your brain that the day has truly begun. Some people incorporate additives like lemon or a pinch of salt for additional benefits, but even plain water has a remarkable impact. This small, consistent act becomes a ritual of care, reminding you that your body's needs come first.

Movement in the morning is a game-changer for energy and focus. It doesn't have to involve an intense workout; even light stretching, yoga, or a brisk walk can invigorate your body and mind. Physical activity triggers the release of endorphins and improves circulation, setting a positive tone for the day. For those who prefer structured exercise, morning workouts often eliminate the risk of skipping it later due to unexpected interruptions. However, the key is consistency rather than intensity. Regular movement, no matter how modest, creates a rhythm that carries through the day.

Mental clarity is equally important in a morning routine. Taking time to center your thoughts and set intentions can significantly enhance focus and productivity. Practices like journaling or meditation are particularly effective for this. Journaling allows you to unload any lingering thoughts from the previous day, organize your priorities, and reflect on what matters most. Meditation, on the other hand, trains your mind to stay present and reduces the mental chatter that can derail your focus. Even a few minutes of mindfulness can create a sense of calm that lasts well into the day.

Another vital component is nourishment. A balanced breakfast fuels both your body and brain, providing the energy needed to tackle the day's demands. Whether you prefer a quick smoothie, a hearty bowl of oats, or simply a piece of fruit, the act of eating mindfully in the morning reinforces the habit of prioritizing your well-being. Skipping breakfast or opting for sugary, processed options can lead to energy crashes and diminished focus, undermining the foundation you're trying to build.

Strategic planning doesn't have to be confined to calendars or to-do lists. Mornings offer a unique opportunity to reflect on your broader goals and align your actions with your intentions. Use this time to identify your top priorities for the day and visualize what success looks like. This could mean jotting down three key tasks you want to accomplish or mentally rehearsing an important presentation. When you start the day with clarity about what matters most, you're less likely to get sidetracked by minor distractions or reactive tasks.

While a morning routine is deeply personal, consistency is what makes it powerful. It's tempting to overhaul your entire schedule and pack it with ambitious practices, but this often leads to burnout or frustration. Instead, introduce one small change at a time, allowing it to become a habit before adding another layer. For instance, if you're not used to exercising in the morning, start with five minutes of stretching rather than committing to a full workout. This gradual approach ensures that your routine remains sustainable and enjoyable.

Sleep is the unsung hero of every effective morning. No routine, no matter how well-crafted, can compensate for inadequate rest. Prioritizing quality sleep is essential for waking up energized and ready to engage with your morning practices. This means setting a consistent bedtime, creating a relaxing pre-sleep ritual, and minimizing disruptions such as excessive screen time or caffeine late in the day. Think of sleep as the foundation upon which your morning routine is built; without it, even the best-laid plans can falter.

Flexibility is another key element. Life is unpredictable, and rigid routines are more likely to crumble under the pressure of unexpected events. A powerful morning routine adapts to your needs and circumstances. This might mean shortening your meditation practice on busy days or swapping a workout for extra sleep when your body needs rest. The goal is not perfection but consistency, even if that means scaling back occasionally. By allowing room for flexibility, you create a routine that supports you rather than constrains you.

Eliminating distractions is crucial to preserving the integrity of your morning. It's all too easy to let notifications, emails, or social media hijack your attention before you've even had a chance to focus on yourself. Consider implementing a "digital-free" period during your morning routine, where you intentionally avoid screens to safeguard your mental clarity. This practice not only enhances productivity but also fosters a sense of control over your time and energy.

Accountability can help solidify your routine. Sharing your intentions with a friend, partner, or accountability group adds a layer of commitment that makes it easier to stay consistent. For example, agreeing to meet a friend for a morning walk or checking in with a mentor about your journaling practice creates external motivation to follow through. Over time, the routine becomes internalized, but accountability can be a helpful bridge in the early stages of forming new habits.

Reflection at the end of the day can enhance your morning routine's effectiveness. Taking a few moments to evaluate what worked well and what felt challenging provides valuable insights for improvement. For example, if you notice that you frequently skip breakfast due to time constraints, you might prepare a simple meal the night before. This iterative process ensures that your routine continues to evolve and serve your needs.

Harnessing the Role of Momentum in Daily Action

Momentum is an invisible force that propels action forward, often making the difference between stagnation and progress. It is not a mystical or uncontrollable phenomenon but a tool that can be harnessed intentionally. When understood and applied correctly, momentum becomes a powerful ally in achieving goals and maintaining consistency in daily actions. It allows you to build on small successes, overcome inertia, and sustain energy as you move through tasks and challenges. Far from being reserved for extraordinary circumstances, momentum is something you can cultivate in the ordinary rhythm of daily life.

At its core, momentum begins with initiation. The hardest part of any task is often the beginning. Newton's first law of motion states that an object at rest stays at rest unless acted upon by an external force. The same principle applies to human behavior. Procrastination, hesitation, or fear of failure can keep you immobilized, staring at the daunting mountain of work ahead. The solution is deceptively simple: start small. Taking even the tiniest action creates a ripple effect, breaking the paralysis of inaction. For example, if you're struggling to begin a daunting project, commit to working on it for just five minutes. Often, this initial push generates enough momentum to keep going far beyond those first few minutes.

Momentum thrives on consistency. Small, repeated actions build energy over time, much like a snowball rolling downhill gathers mass and speed. Consistency doesn't mean perfection; it means showing up regularly, even when circumstances aren't ideal. Consider a writer working on a book. Writing a few hundred words every day might seem insignificant in the moment, but over weeks and months, those words accumulate into chapters and eventually a completed manuscript. The key is to focus on progress rather than perfection, understanding that momentum is built through persistence rather than grand gestures.

One of the most effective ways to maintain momentum is by celebrating small wins. Achieving a small milestone generates a sense of accomplishment, releasing dopamine in the brain and reinforcing positive behavior. These moments of recognition act as fuel, motivating you to continue. For instance, if you're trying to adopt a new fitness routine, acknowledging the effort of completing your first week, even if it's just a series of short workouts, can be enough to keep you moving forward. The celebration doesn't have to be elaborate—it could be as simple as pausing to acknowledge your progress or rewarding yourself with something meaningful. What matters is that you take a moment to recognize the effort you've invested.

Momentum can also be amplified by creating a sequence of actions that flow seamlessly into one another. This is often referred to as "habit stacking." By linking a new behavior to an existing habit, you reduce the friction of starting something new. For example, if you want to build a meditation practice, you could tie it to a habit you already have, like brushing your teeth. Each time you finish brushing, you would immediately sit for five minutes of meditation. This linkage creates a chain reaction, allowing one action to naturally lead into the next. Over time, the sequence becomes automatic, eliminating the need for conscious decision-making and preserving your mental energy for other tasks.

Your environment plays a critical role in sustaining momentum. A cluttered or disorganized space can create mental resistance, while a well-designed environment can make it easier to stay on track. For example, if you're trying to establish a habit of reading every evening, keeping a book within arm's reach of your favorite chair removes a barrier to starting. Similarly, if you're working toward healthier eating habits, having pre-portioned snacks readily available makes the choice simpler and more appealing. By minimizing obstacles and designing your surroundings to align with your goals, you create conditions where momentum can thrive.

Energy management is another essential element. Momentum falters when you're physically or mentally depleted. Paying attention to your energy levels throughout the day allows you to align your most demanding tasks with your peak performance periods. For many people, this means tackling high-priority work in the morning when focus and willpower are strongest. However, everyone's energy patterns are different, and understanding your own rhythms is key. Breaks are equally important; they allow you to recharge and prevent burnout, ensuring that momentum is sustainable rather than a short-lived burst.

The power of momentum also lies in its ability to build confidence. Each small success reinforces the belief that you are capable of achieving more. This growing confidence creates a positive feedback loop: the more you accomplish, the more motivated you become to tackle the next challenge. Over time, this builds a sense of competence and self-efficacy that spills over into other areas of life. For instance, someone who successfully completes a month-long fitness challenge might find themselves feeling more confident in unrelated areas, such as their career or personal relationships. Momentum, once established, has a way of creating ripple effects far beyond its initial focus.

It's important to recognize that momentum can be fragile if not nurtured. Disruptions, setbacks, or distractions can derail progress, making it harder to regain your footing. One way to protect momentum is by creating contingency plans for inevitable obstacles. For example, if you're working on a daily writing habit, decide in advance how you'll handle days when time is short—perhaps by committing to write just one sentence instead of skipping altogether. These contingency measures ensure that even when circumstances aren't ideal, you can maintain some level of progress, preventing the complete loss of momentum.

Accountability is a powerful tool for sustaining momentum. Sharing your goals and progress with someone else creates an external layer of motivation. Whether it's a friend, mentor, or accountability group, having someone to check in with can keep you focused and committed. For instance, a person training for a marathon might find it easier to stick to their running schedule if they're part of a running club or have a training partner. The social element adds a layer of encouragement and support that makes it easier to push through challenges.

Momentum can also be reignited when it stalls. Everyone experiences periods where progress slows or stops altogether. When this happens, it's important to return to the basics: start small, focus on one task at a time, and allow the process to rebuild naturally. For example, if you've fallen out of a routine, don't try to jump back in at full speed. Instead, reintroduce the habit in a manageable way, such as committing to just five minutes of action. This approach reduces the pressure to perform perfectly and allows momentum to build gradually.

Intrinsic motivation plays a crucial role in maintaining momentum. When your actions are driven by internal desires rather than external rewards, it becomes easier to sustain effort over the long term. Reflect on why your goals matter to you and how they align with your values. This deeper connection provides a wellspring of motivation that fuels momentum even when external circumstances are discouraging. For example, someone pursuing a creative project might find inspiration in the joy of self-expression rather than focusing solely on the end result.

Momentum is not just about speed; it's about direction. Moving quickly in the wrong direction can lead to frustration and wasted effort, while deliberate, purposeful action ensures that progress is meaningful.

Periodic reflection allows you to assess whether your momentum is aligned with your goals. Are you making progress toward what truly matters, or are you simply staying busy? This kind of recalibration ensures that your energy is being channeled effectively, maximizing the impact of your efforts.

Chapter 6: The Art of Focus and Prioritization

Eliminating Distractions The Myth of Multitasking

Distractions are the silent thieves of productivity, stealing your focus and sabotaging meaningful progress. They creep in through notifications, endless scrolling, fragmented work environments, and even the illusion of doing many things simultaneously. At first glance, multitasking appears to be the perfect antidote to a busy world—a way to juggle multiple responsibilities and maximize efficiency. Yet, it is often a myth, one that dilutes your attention and leaves you with half-finished tasks and a growing sense of frustration. Eliminating distractions and debunking the multitasking myth are essential steps toward reclaiming your time and channeling your energy into what truly matters.

The brain is not wired to multitask effectively. While it may seem like you're handling multiple tasks at once, what you're actually doing is task-switching—rapidly shifting focus from one thing to another. Each switch imposes a cognitive cost, as your brain must reorient itself to the new task. This process consumes mental energy and reduces efficiency, making even simple tasks take longer than they would if tackled individually. For example, consider the common scenario of answering emails while participating in a virtual meeting. You're not truly engaging with either; instead, your brain is bouncing between the two, missing important details and producing subpar results.

Research supports this reality. Studies have shown that multitasking can reduce productivity by up to 40%, as the mental effort required to switch tasks creates delays and increases the likelihood of errors. Beyond productivity, multitasking also impairs memory retention. When your attention is divided, information is less likely to be encoded into long-term memory. This can leave you feeling scattered and struggling to recall details or follow through on commitments.

Distractions amplify the inefficiency of multitasking. Every time your phone buzzes or a notification pops up on your screen, your focus is disrupted. Even if you don't immediately act on the distraction, the mere awareness of it pulls your attention away from the task at hand. It takes an average of 23 minutes and 15 seconds to fully regain focus after an interruption, according to studies. Multiply that by the number of distractions in a typical day, and it becomes clear why so many people feel perpetually busy yet unproductive.

The first step in eliminating distractions is identifying their sources. Some are external, like noisy coworkers, social media, or cluttered workspaces. Others are internal, rooted in habits, emotional states, or mental patterns. For example, procrastination often masquerades as multitasking, as you jump between tasks to avoid the discomfort of fully committing to one. Understanding the nature of your distractions allows you to address them more effectively.

Creating a distraction-free environment is crucial for deep focus. This might involve physical adjustments, such as decluttering your workspace, using noise-canceling headphones, or setting up a dedicated area for work. It could also mean technological interventions, like turning off notifications, enabling "Do Not Disturb" modes, or using apps designed to block distracting websites. These changes signal to your brain that this is a space for concentration, not for mindless wandering.

Time-blocking is another powerful strategy to combat distractions and the inefficiency of multitasking. By dedicating specific blocks of time to particular tasks, you create structure and reduce the temptation to switch between activities. For instance, you might allocate the first hour of your morning to strategic planning, followed by a focused work session, then a designated period for responding to emails. Knowing that each task has its place reduces the anxiety of trying to manage everything at once, allowing you to give your full attention to the task at hand.

The concept of single-tasking, or deep work, is an antidote to the myth of multitasking. Single-tasking involves immersing yourself fully in one activity, free from interruptions or competing demands. This approach not only enhances productivity but also fosters a sense of satisfaction and accomplishment. When your attention is undivided, you can produce higher-quality work, solve problems more creatively, and experience a state of flow—a mental state where focus and performance peak. For example, a writer who dedicates uninterrupted time to drafting an article is likely to produce clearer, more compelling content than one who alternates between writing, checking emails, and scrolling through social media.

Mindfulness plays a significant role in resisting distractions and embracing single-tasking. Developing awareness of your attention allows you to notice when it begins to wander and gently bring it back to the present moment. This skill is especially valuable in a world designed to pull your focus in countless directions. Practicing mindfulness doesn't require elaborate rituals; it can be as simple as pausing to take a few deep breaths or setting an intention before starting a task. Over time, this practice strengthens your ability to concentrate and reduces the hold distractions have over your mind.

Accountability can also be a powerful tool. Sharing your goals or tasks with someone else creates a sense of external commitment, reducing the likelihood of succumbing to distractions. For instance, if you've promised a colleague that you'll deliver a report by the end of the day, you're more likely to stay focused on that task rather than getting sidetracked. Similarly, working in an environment where others are engaged in focused tasks—such as a library or co-working space—can reinforce your own commitment to avoiding distractions.

Internal distractions, such as self-doubt, perfectionism, or overthinking, require a different approach. These mental barriers often stem from fear or uncertainty, making it tempting to seek out distractions as a way to avoid confronting them. Overcoming these challenges involves cultivating self-compassion and recognizing that progress is more important than perfection. For example, if you find yourself procrastinating because you're worried about making mistakes, remind yourself that taking imperfect action is better than taking no action at all. Shifting your mindset in this way reduces the emotional pull of distractions and helps you stay engaged with your work.

Digital detoxing is another strategy to consider. The constant barrage of notifications, updates, and alerts from devices can create a sense of urgency that disrupts focus. Setting boundaries around technology use—such as scheduling specific times to check emails or turning off notifications during work hours—helps create mental space for concentration. Some people find it helpful to designate "phone-free" zones or times, such as during meals or before bed, to reinforce the habit of being present and undistracted.

It's important to acknowledge that not all distractions are avoidable. Life is unpredictable, and interruptions will inevitably occur. The goal is not to eliminate every distraction but to build resilience and strategies for quickly regaining focus when they arise. For example, if a coworker interrupts you with a question, you might respond briefly and then use a quick mental reset—such as taking a deep breath or reviewing your task list—to refocus on your work. These small recovery techniques prevent distractions from derailing your momentum entirely.

The myth of multitasking persists because it appeals to our desire to be efficient and capable of handling many responsibilities. However, the reality is that true efficiency comes from focus and intentionality. By eliminating distractions and embracing single-tasking, you create the conditions for deeper engagement, higher-quality work, and a greater sense of accomplishment. The shift away from multitasking may feel uncomfortable at first, especially if you're accustomed to juggling multiple demands. But with practice and persistence, it becomes a habit that transforms not only how you work but also how you experience your time and energy.

Mastering the Eisenhower Matrix to Prioritize Tasks

Every day presents a flurry of tasks vying for your attention, each one seemingly urgent, important, or both. Without a clear framework for prioritization, it's easy to feel overwhelmed, unsure of where to begin and what truly deserves your energy. The Eisenhower Matrix, named after former U.S. President Dwight D. Eisenhower, offers a practical and effective way to cut through this chaos. By separating tasks based on urgency and importance, it provides clarity and helps you focus on what matters most while avoiding the trap of perpetual busyness.

The Eisenhower Matrix is built on a deceptively simple structure: a four-quadrant grid. The rows divide tasks into "Important" and "Not Important," while the columns split them into "Urgent" and "Not Urgent." Together, these distinctions create four categories of tasks: important and urgent, important but not urgent, urgent but not important, and neither urgent nor important. Each category requires a different approach, and mastering this framework is key to making deliberate choices about how to allocate your time.

The first quadrant, important and urgent, represents tasks that demand immediate attention. These are crises, deadlines, or pressing matters that cannot be delayed without serious consequences. For example, a leaking pipe that's flooding your home or a work project due in a few hours falls into this category. While it's inevitable that some tasks will land here, the goal is to minimize their frequency. Living predominantly in this quadrant leads to constant firefighting, leaving little room for strategic thinking or long-term planning. To reduce the dominance of this category in your life, it's essential to identify and address root causes. For instance, poor planning, procrastination, or neglecting important but not urgent tasks can cause preventable crises to escalate into this quadrant.

The second quadrant, important but not urgent, is where the magic happens. This is the realm of proactive, high-value activities that contribute to your long-term goals and well-being. Examples include strategic planning, personal development, exercise, and nurturing relationships. These tasks don't demand immediate action, which makes them easy to postpone. However, neglecting them can have significant consequences over time, as opportunities are missed and problems are allowed to fester. Regularly investing time in this quadrant reduces the likelihood of crises in the first quadrant, creating a virtuous cycle of productivity and balance. To maximize the impact of this category, schedule these tasks intentionally, treating them with the same level of commitment as urgent deadlines.

The third quadrant, urgent but not important, consists of tasks that feel pressing but ultimately add little value. These are often interruptions, distractions, or obligations that are imposed by others. For instance, an unexpected phone call during a focused work session or attending a meeting that could have been an email exemplifies this category. While these tasks may require immediate attention, they often detract from more meaningful work. The key to managing this quadrant is learning to delegate, decline, or delay tasks that don't align with your priorities. For example, if a colleague asks for assistance with a low-priority task, consider whether someone else is better suited to handle it or whether it can wait until you've completed more critical work.

The final quadrant, neither urgent nor important, represents time-wasters. These are activities that contribute nothing to your goals or well-being, such as excessive social media scrolling, binge-watching television, or mindlessly checking emails. While occasional leisure and relaxation are essential, spending too much time in this quadrant leads to stagnation and frustration. Eliminating or significantly reducing these tasks frees up time and energy for more meaningful pursuits. To do this, it's important to identify your personal distractions and set boundaries around them. For example, you might limit social media use to specific times of day or designate certain hours as screen-free zones.

Applying the Eisenhower Matrix in daily life begins with a clear understanding of your priorities. Before categorizing tasks, take a moment to reflect on what truly matters to you—both professionally and personally. What are your long-term goals? What values guide your decisions? This clarity serves as a compass, ensuring that your actions align with your larger purpose. For example, if one of your goals is to improve your physical health, tasks like meal planning, exercise, and regular check-ups should consistently appear in the important but not urgent quadrant.

Once you've identified your priorities, create a habit of sorting tasks into the matrix. This can be done daily, weekly, or even in the moment when new tasks arise. Start by listing everything you need to do and then categorizing each item into the appropriate quadrant. Be honest with yourself during this process; it's easy to label tasks as urgent when they are merely convenient or comfortable. For example, responding immediately to a non-critical email may feel productive, but it often belongs in the urgent but not important quadrant.

Using the matrix effectively requires more than categorization—it demands action. For tasks in the important and urgent quadrant, focus on resolving them as quickly and efficiently as possible. This often means dropping less critical activities to give these tasks your full attention. For important but not urgent tasks, schedule dedicated time to work on them, treating them as non-negotiable appointments. For urgent but not important tasks, delegate or defer wherever possible, and for tasks in the neither urgent nor important quadrant, eliminate or limit them ruthlessly.

Time-blocking can enhance the implementation of the Eisenhower Matrix. By assigning specific periods to each quadrant, you ensure that all categories receive appropriate attention. For example, you might reserve mornings for important but not urgent tasks, when your energy and focus are at their peak. Afternoons could be dedicated to resolving urgent and important matters, while the end of the day might be used for addressing urgent but not important tasks. This structured approach prevents less critical activities from encroaching on high-value work.

The Eisenhower Matrix also highlights the importance of boundaries. To protect your focus and energy, it's essential to say no to tasks that don't align with your priorities. This might mean declining unnecessary meetings, pushing back on unreasonable requests, or limiting access to your time. While it can be uncomfortable to set boundaries, doing so reinforces your commitment to what matters most. For example, if a coworker frequently interrupts you with non-urgent questions, establish a designated time for addressing their concerns rather than allowing constant interruptions.

Reflection and adjustment are integral to mastering the matrix. Periodically review how you're spending your time and assess whether your actions align with your priorities. Are you investing enough energy in the important but not urgent quadrant, or are you getting bogged down by urgent but not important tasks? Are there recurring crises in the important and urgent quadrant that could be prevented through better planning? Use these insights to refine your approach, making small adjustments as needed.

The beauty of the Eisenhower Matrix lies in its flexibility and adaptability. It's not a rigid system but a tool that evolves with your needs and circumstances. Whether you're managing a busy work schedule, balancing personal commitments, or pursuing ambitious goals, the matrix provides a framework for intentional action. By consistently applying its principles, you shift from reactive to proactive, gaining control over your time and energy.

Chapter 7: Sustaining Motivation Over Time

Intrinsic vs Extrinsic Motivation What Drives You

Motivation is the engine that powers action, the invisible force pushing you to pursue goals, confront challenges, and make decisions. Yet, not all motivation operates the same way. It comes in two distinct forms: intrinsic and extrinsic. Understanding the difference between these two types—and how they influence behavior—can unlock a deeper comprehension of what truly drives you. Furthermore, knowing how to cultivate the right balance between the two ensures that your efforts align with long-term fulfillment rather than temporary satisfaction.

Intrinsic motivation originates from within. It's the kind of drive fueled by genuine interest, passion, or enjoyment of an activity itself, rather than by any external reward or consequence. When you feel intrinsically motivated, the task at hand becomes its own reward. Think of an artist lost in the act of painting, not for accolades or financial gain, but for the sheer joy of creation. Or consider the curious mind diving into books and research, not because of a looming deadline but out of a thirst for knowledge. Intrinsic motivation thrives on personal satisfaction and the alignment between actions and inner values.

Extrinsic motivation, on the other hand, is driven by external factors. These might include rewards like money, recognition, promotions, or even avoidance of negative consequences such as punishment or criticism. For instance, an employee working overtime to secure a bonus or a student studying late into the night to achieve a high grade are both examples of extrinsically motivated behavior. The focus here is on the outcome rather than the process, with external validation serving as the primary driver of action.

Neither form of motivation is inherently better or worse. Both can be effective in different contexts, and their influence often exists along a spectrum rather than as two rigidly separated categories. However, their impact on performance, satisfaction, and persistence can vary significantly. Intrinsic motivation is often associated with higher-quality work, deeper engagement, and long-term commitment. When you're intrinsically driven, obstacles feel less daunting, and the work itself becomes a source of energy. On the flip side, extrinsic motivation can be a powerful tool for initiating action, especially when tackling tasks that may not inherently spark joy or interest. For example, extrinsic rewards can motivate you to complete a mundane but necessary chore, like filing taxes or organizing paperwork.

The balance between intrinsic and extrinsic motivation is delicate. Over-reliance on external rewards can sometimes undermine intrinsic motivation, a phenomenon known as the overjustification effect. When an activity that was once enjoyable for its own sake becomes associated with external rewards, the internal drive can diminish. For example, a child who loves drawing might lose interest if they begin receiving monetary rewards for every piece of artwork. The shift in focus—

from personal enjoyment to earning a reward—can rob the activity of its original appeal.

Similarly, extrinsic motivation alone may lead to burnout or dissatisfaction if the external rewards fail to align with deeper personal values. A person who spends years climbing the corporate ladder for financial gain might eventually feel unfulfilled if their work lacks meaning or purpose. This disconnect between external success and internal satisfaction underscores the importance of integrating intrinsic motivators into your pursuits.

So, what drives you? Identifying the root of your motivation begins with self-reflection. Consider a goal or activity you're currently pursuing. Are you doing it because it excites and fulfills you, or because of the rewards and recognition it promises? Perhaps it's a mix of both. For instance, someone training for a marathon might be intrinsically motivated by the challenge and self-discipline it represents, while also being extrinsically motivated by the pride of crossing the finish line in front of friends and family. Recognizing the blend of these forces allows you to better understand what sustains your efforts and what might need adjustment.

Cultivating intrinsic motivation often involves connecting with your core values and interests. When you align your actions with what genuinely matters to you, motivation becomes more sustainable. This might mean reframing tasks to see their deeper purpose or finding ways to make them more enjoyable. For example, if exercising feels like a chore, focusing on the benefits it provides—such as increased energy, improved mood, or the chance to explore nature—can shift your perspective and ignite a sense of intrinsic motivation.

Developing curiosity is another way to foster intrinsic motivation. When you approach tasks with a sense of wonder or a desire to learn, they become opportunities for growth rather than obligations. For instance, instead of dreading a challenging work assignment, view it as a chance to develop new skills or expand your knowledge. This mindset shift transforms the activity into a source of personal enrichment, making it easier to stay engaged and committed.

On the other hand, leveraging extrinsic motivation effectively requires setting clear, meaningful rewards that reinforce desired behaviors without overshadowing intrinsic motivators. For example, using a reward system to encourage consistency in a new habit—such as treating yourself to a small indulgence after a week of regular exercise—can help you stay on track without diminishing the intrinsic benefits of the activity. The key is to ensure that external rewards complement, rather than replace, internal satisfaction.

Accountability can also serve as a form of extrinsic motivation, providing structure and encouragement when intrinsic motivation wanes. Sharing your goals with a trusted friend, mentor, or group creates a sense of responsibility that can help you push through moments of doubt or fatigue. For example, someone training for a fitness goal might join a workout group or hire a coach to stay motivated and focused. The external support provides an additional layer of motivation while still allowing personal fulfillment to take center stage.

It's worth noting that motivation is not static. It ebbs and flows, influenced by context, emotions, and external circumstances. What motivates you today might not motivate you tomorrow, and that's okay. The key is to remain adaptable, recognizing when your approach needs to shift. For example, if extrinsic rewards no longer feel satisfying, it might be time to reconnect with the intrinsic value of your work. Conversely, if intrinsic motivation starts to waver, introducing external incentives can provide a temporary boost to reignite your drive.

Understanding the interplay between intrinsic and extrinsic motivation also allows you to inspire and influence others. Whether you're a leader, teacher, parent, or mentor, recognizing what drives those around you can help you tailor your approach to their needs. For instance, a manager seeking to motivate their team might focus on creating an environment where employees feel valued and engaged, balancing external rewards like bonuses with opportunities for personal growth and creative expression.

The Role of Rewards and Accountability Partners

Rewards and accountability partners are two powerful tools that can significantly enhance the journey toward achieving goals. They operate on the principle of external reinforcement, tapping into both psychological and social influences to sustain momentum, encourage consistency, and provide a sense of accomplishment. While intrinsic motivation often fuels the initial desire to pursue a goal, external mechanisms like rewards and accountability partners serve to bridge the gap between intention and action, especially during moments of fatigue, doubt, or distraction. Leveraging these tools effectively requires a thoughtful approach that aligns them with your personal goals and values, ensuring they complement rather than undermine your long-term efforts.

Rewards are deeply ingrained in human behavior. From an early age, we learn that certain actions lead to positive outcomes, creating a feedback loop that reinforces those behaviors. In adulthood, the same principle holds true: when we associate effort with a tangible or intangible reward, we're more likely to repeat the behavior. However, the key to using rewards effectively lies in their design. A poorly chosen reward can feel hollow or even counterproductive, while a well-designed one can create a powerful incentive to push forward.

The most effective rewards are those that align with the nature of the goal and the preferences of the individual. For example, someone working toward a fitness milestone might reward themselves with new workout gear or a relaxing massage—tangible treats that directly relate to their progress. On the other hand, intangible rewards, like taking time for a favorite hobby or enjoying a quiet day off, can be equally motivating, especially for those who value experiences over possessions. The critical factor is that the reward feels meaningful and proportional to the effort invested.

It's also important to establish a clear connection between the reward and the achievement of specific milestones. Vague or inconsistent rewards can dilute their impact, making them less effective over time. For instance, if the goal is to write a chapter of a book, setting a concrete reward for completing the draft—such as enjoying a night out or indulging in a favorite dessert—creates a clear incentive to stay committed. This specificity not only provides motivation but also fosters a sense of satisfaction and progress when the reward is earned.

While rewards can be motivating, they must be used carefully to avoid creating dependency. Over-reliance on external rewards may shift focus away from the intrinsic value of the activity, reducing long-term engagement. To prevent this, rewards should complement intrinsic motivation rather than replace it. For example, someone who loves running should view a reward, like a new pair of running shoes, as an enhancement of their passion rather than the sole reason for lacing up their sneakers. By reinforcing the inherent enjoyment or purpose of the activity, rewards can sustain motivation without undermining its deeper roots.

Accountability partners, on the other hand, introduce a social dimension to goal-setting and execution. Humans are inherently social creatures, and the presence of another person invested in your success can have a profound impact on your behavior. An accountability partner serves as a mirror, reflecting your goals, progress, and challenges, while also providing encouragement, perspective, and a sense of shared responsibility.

The effectiveness of an accountability partner lies in the mutual commitment to regular check-ins and honest communication. This relationship creates a structure that helps you stay aligned with your intentions, even when motivation wanes. For example, a person aiming to develop a daily meditation practice might partner with a friend who shares the same goal. By setting a schedule to discuss their progress and challenges, both individuals benefit from the shared accountability, making it harder to skip sessions without feeling a sense of responsibility.

The choice of accountability partner is crucial. Not everyone is suited to this role, and selecting the wrong person can undermine the process. An effective accountability partner is someone who understands your goals, respects your boundaries, and provides constructive feedback without judgment. They should also share a level of commitment to the process, ensuring that the partnership remains balanced and mutually beneficial. For instance, a colleague who is also striving to improve time management might be an ideal partner for sharing tips, progress updates, and encouragement.

Technology can also play a role in facilitating accountability. Apps, virtual groups, and online communities provide platforms for tracking progress and connecting with others who share similar goals. For example, someone training for a marathon might join an online running group where members share their weekly mileage and encourage one another. These digital tools expand the scope of accountability, making it accessible even for those who may not have a suitable partner in their immediate circle.

The combination of rewards and accountability partners can be particularly powerful when used together. While rewards provide a personal incentive to achieve milestones, accountability partners introduce an external layer of commitment that reinforces consistency. For instance, someone working toward a weight loss goal might set a personal reward for reaching a target weight, such as purchasing new clothes, while also partnering with a friend to attend weekly fitness classes. The interplay between these two mechanisms creates a dynamic system of reinforcement that addresses both internal and external motivators.

However, the role of accountability partners extends beyond simply tracking progress. They can also serve as a source of emotional support during setbacks or challenges. Goals are rarely achieved in a linear fashion, and moments of doubt or frustration are inevitable. In these moments, an accountability partner can provide perspective, remind you of your progress, and help you refocus on your larger purpose. For example, a writer struggling with creative block might turn to their accountability partner for encouragement or brainstorming, reigniting their enthusiasm for the project.

Flexibility is an essential component of both rewards and accountability partnerships. Goals and circumstances evolve, and it's important to adapt these mechanisms accordingly. For example, as you make progress toward your goal, you might find that certain rewards no longer feel motivating or that your accountability partner's availability has changed. Regularly reassessing and adjusting these systems ensures that they remain effective and aligned with your needs.

While rewards and accountability partners are valuable tools, they are not substitutes for personal commitment or effort. At their core, they function as supports, enhancing your ability to stay on track and persevere through challenges. However, the ultimate responsibility for achieving your goals lies with you. By integrating these tools into your routine thoughtfully and intentionally, you create a framework that amplifies your motivation and increases the likelihood of success.

Navigating Plateaus and Avoiding Burnout

Progress is rarely linear. Whether you're working toward personal goals, professional milestones, or physical achievements, there comes a time when the momentum slows, and the results seem stagnant. These moments, often referred to as plateaus, can be frustrating and demoralizing. They have the power to make you question your methods, your dedication, and even the feasibility of your ambitions. Compounding this challenge is the ever-present risk of burnout, a state of emotional, mental, and physical exhaustion that can derail even the most determined individuals. Navigating these obstacles requires not only resilience but also a strategy that balances persistence with self-care.

Plateaus occur for various reasons, and understanding why they happen is the first step in overcoming them. Sometimes, they're the natural result of adaptation. For example, when pursuing fitness goals, your body becomes accustomed to a routine over time, leading to diminished returns despite consistent effort. The same principle applies to mental and professional endeavors. If your brain or habits settle into a rhythm, growth slows, and progress feels imperceptible. Plateaus can also stem from external factors—limited resources, unforeseen circumstances, or even environmental changes that impact your ability to perform. Regardless of the cause, the frustration of putting in effort without visible results can shake your confidence and test your patience.

The key to breaking through a plateau lies in making adjustments rather than abandoning your goals. If you find yourself stuck, start by evaluating your current approach. Are you repeating the same methods without variation? Have you overlooked opportunities to challenge yourself or step outside your comfort zone? For example, if a writer feels uninspired after months of adhering to a rigid writing schedule, experimenting with a new genre or setting might reignite creativity. Similarly, someone stuck in a weight-loss plateau could try altering their workout intensity or exploring different forms of exercise to stimulate progress. Plateaus often signal a need for change, and even small adjustments can have a cascading effect that revitalizes momentum.

Tracking progress in detail can also shed light on the factors contributing to a plateau. When goals feel distant, it's easy to overlook incremental improvements that are happening beneath the surface. Keeping a record of your efforts—whether through a journal, spreadsheet, or app—helps you identify patterns, trends, and overlooked successes. For instance, someone learning a new language might feel stagnant after a few months, but revisiting their notes could reveal marked improvement in vocabulary and comprehension. Recognizing these smaller victories builds confidence and reinforces the idea that progress is still occurring, even if it's less visible.

However, plateaus are not solely about the mechanics of effort; they're also deeply tied to mindset. Comparing yourself to others, setting unrealistic expectations, or fixating on perfection can amplify the frustration of feeling stuck. Remember that progress is deeply individual, shaped by your unique circumstances and pace. Instead of focusing on what hasn't been achieved, shift your attention to what has. Gratitude and reflection on past successes create a positive framework for tackling the present challenge. Reframing your mindset from "I'm failing" to "I'm learning" transforms the plateau from an obstacle into an opportunity for growth.

While plateaus test your patience, burnout threatens your capacity to continue entirely. Burnout often occurs when you push yourself relentlessly without allowing time for rest or recovery. It manifests as exhaustion, diminished enthusiasm, and a sense of being overwhelmed. The irony of burnout is that it often strikes those who are most passionate and driven, as they push themselves beyond their limits in pursuit of excellence. Recognizing the signs of burnout early is crucial to addressing it before it derails your progress.

One of the most effective ways to prevent burnout is to incorporate regular breaks and downtime into your routine. Rest is not a luxury; it's a necessity for sustained performance. Overworking yourself might yield short-term results, but it's unsustainable in the long run. For example, a student preparing for exams might feel compelled to study for hours on end, but research shows that breaks improve focus and retention. Scheduling time for relaxation, hobbies, and social connections ensures that your mind and body have the chance to recharge, making you more resilient in the face of challenges.

Setting boundaries is another crucial strategy for avoiding burnout. In a world that often glorifies hustle culture, it's easy to internalize the belief that success requires constant effort. However, this mindset neglects the importance of balance. Learn to say no to demands that don't align with your priorities and delegate tasks when possible. For instance, a professional juggling multiple responsibilities might delegate non-essential tasks to colleagues or outsource certain duties to create space for more meaningful work. Protecting your time and energy allows you to focus on what truly matters, reducing the risk of spreading yourself too thin.

Variety is equally important in combating burnout. Monotony can sap enthusiasm, making even the most exciting goals feel like a chore. Incorporating new experiences, challenges, or perspectives keeps your efforts fresh and engaging. For example, if you're pursuing a creative project, stepping away to explore a different medium or activity can spark new ideas. Similarly, someone stuck in a professional rut might benefit from attending workshops, networking events, or seeking mentorship to reignite their passion. Variety doesn't mean abandoning your goals; it means approaching them from different angles to maintain enthusiasm and curiosity.

Self-compassion plays a pivotal role in navigating both plateaus and burnout. It's easy to fall into the trap of self-criticism when progress stalls or energy wanes, but this only exacerbates the problem. Treat yourself with the same kindness and understanding you would offer a friend in similar circumstances. Acknowledge that setbacks are a natural part of any journey and that rest is not a sign of weakness but a necessary step toward resilience. For example, if a musician struggles to compose after weeks of practice, taking time to relax and reflect might provide the clarity needed to move forward.

Support systems are another invaluable resource during these challenging periods. Sharing your struggles with trusted friends, family, or mentors can provide perspective, encouragement, and advice. Sometimes, an outside perspective reveals solutions or insights that you might have overlooked. For example, a business owner feeling stuck in expansion plans might gain fresh ideas from discussing challenges with a mentor who has faced similar hurdles. Surrounding yourself with people who believe in your potential reinforces your own belief in your ability to overcome obstacles.

Finally, revisit your "why." When progress slows or burnout looms, reconnecting with the deeper purpose behind your goals can reignite motivation. Ask yourself why you started this journey in the first place. What does success look like to you, and how will achieving it enhance your life or the lives of others? For example, an educator struggling with fatigue might find renewed energy by reflecting on the impact their work has on students' growth and futures. Anchoring your efforts in a meaningful purpose provides the emotional fuel needed to persevere through difficult times.

Chapter 8: The Discipline of Time Management

Time Blocking Structuring Your Day for Maximum Efficiency

Time is one of the few resources that is both finite and universally distributed. Everyone, regardless of their circumstances, has the same twenty-four hours in each day. The difference between those who thrive and those who struggle often comes down to how effectively those hours are managed. Time blocking is a method that transforms chaotic days into structured, purpose-driven schedules. By allocating specific blocks of time to particular tasks or categories, you gain clarity, control, and a greater sense of accomplishment. This approach not only enhances productivity but also reduces stress by eliminating the guesswork of what needs to be done and when.

At its core, time blocking is about intentionality. Instead of reacting to demands as they arise or relying on a disorganized to-do list, you proactively decide how your day will unfold. It's not merely about filling every available moment but about creating a realistic structure that aligns with your goals and priorities. This level of premeditation ensures that what matters most gets the attention it deserves, while less critical tasks are managed without taking over your day.

The first step in implementing time blocking is understanding your commitments and responsibilities. Before you can assign blocks of time, you need a clear picture of what needs to be accomplished. Start by listing all the tasks, activities, and obligations you're juggling. This could include work assignments, personal errands, family responsibilities, and even leisure activities. The goal is to capture everything that competes for your attention, no matter how small or routine it may seem. For instance, a professional might include meetings, project deadlines, and client follow-ups, while also factoring in personal time for exercise, meal preparation, and relaxation.

Once you have a comprehensive list, the next step is prioritization. Not all tasks are created equal, and time blocking works best when it reflects the relative importance of your responsibilities. Identify which tasks are essential, which are important but flexible, and which can be delegated or postponed. For example, preparing for an upcoming presentation might take precedence over sorting through emails, while a recurring household chore could be delegated to a family member or outsourced. This process of prioritization helps you focus your time and energy on what truly matters, rather than getting bogged down by less critical tasks.

With your priorities in place, you can begin designing your time blocks. Start by identifying your peak productivity hours—the times of day when you feel most focused and energetic. For many people, this might be in the morning, before distractions accumulate and energy wanes. These high-value hours should be reserved for your most demanding or creative tasks, such as brainstorming ideas, tackling complex problems, or working on long-term projects.

By aligning your most important work with your natural rhythms, you maximize efficiency and reduce the likelihood of burnout.

It's also important to build flexibility into your schedule. While time blocking provides structure, life is unpredictable, and rigid adherence to a plan can be counterproductive. Leave some open blocks or buffer time between tasks to account for unexpected interruptions, delays, or the need to recalibrate. For instance, if you anticipate back-to-back meetings, scheduling a short break afterward ensures you have time to decompress and refocus before diving into the next activity. Flexibility doesn't mean abandoning structure; it means creating a plan that accommodates the inevitable ebb and flow of daily life.

Another critical aspect of time blocking is accounting for transitions. Tasks don't exist in isolation; moving from one activity to the next takes time, whether it's commuting to a meeting, setting up for a presentation, or simply shifting your mental focus. Failing to account for these transitions can lead to overbooking and unnecessary stress. For example, if you schedule a meeting to end at 11:00 a.m. and another task to start at the same time, you're setting yourself up for frustration. Building in transition time ensures your schedule feels realistic and manageable, rather than rushed and overwhelming.

Time blocking isn't just about work; it's about balance. A well-structured day includes time for both productivity and self-care. Neglecting personal needs in favor of work can lead to burnout and diminished performance over time. Incorporate blocks for activities that recharge you, whether it's exercise, reading, meditation, or spending time with loved ones. For example, dedicating 30 minutes in the evening to unwind with a book not only provides a mental break but also creates a clear boundary between work and personal time. These intentional pauses are just as important as your professional commitments, as they contribute to overall well-being and sustainability.

One of the most common challenges in time blocking is overestimating what can be accomplished in a day. It's tempting to fill every block with ambitious tasks, but this can lead to frustration when reality doesn't match expectations. Aim for a balance between ambition and realism, leaving room for adjustments as needed. For instance, if you consistently find yourself running out of time for certain tasks, consider whether they're too large to fit into a single block and break them into smaller, more manageable steps. This approach not only makes tasks feel less daunting but also provides a sense of progress as each step is completed.

Distractions are another obstacle that can derail even the best-laid plans. In a world filled with constant notifications, emails, and demands for attention, staying focused during a time block requires discipline and intentionality. Create an environment that supports concentration, whether it's by silencing your phone, closing unnecessary browser tabs, or setting boundaries with colleagues and family members. For example, if you've blocked two hours to work on a critical project, let others know you're unavailable during that time and resist the urge to check your email or social media. These small but deliberate actions create the mental space needed to fully engage with the task at hand.

Reviewing and refining your time-blocking strategy is an ongoing process. What works today might not work tomorrow, as goals, priorities, and circumstances evolve. Regularly assess how well your blocks align with your actual needs and make adjustments as necessary. For instance, if you find that certain tasks consistently take longer than expected, allocate more time for them in future schedules. Similarly, if a particular block feels underutilized, consider repurposing it for a different activity. Flexibility and self-awareness are key to maintaining a time-blocking system that remains effective over the long term.

Applying the 80/20 Principle to Focus on What Matters

The 80/20 Principle, also known as the Pareto Principle, is a concept with profound implications for productivity, decision-making, and achieving meaningful results. At its core, the principle suggests that 80% of outcomes often stem from 20% of inputs. While the exact ratio may vary in specific contexts, the takeaway is clear: not all efforts, tasks, or resources yield equal results. Identifying and focusing on the critical 20% that drives the majority of your success can streamline your efforts, save time, and maximize impact. This principle urges you to move away from the notion that every task holds equal importance and instead concentrate on what truly matters.

In practice, applying the 80/20 Principle requires a shift in perspective. It means taking a hard look at your workload, responsibilities, and priorities to discern where your energy is best spent. Start by analyzing your current activities. Whether you're managing a business, working toward personal development, or juggling a variety of commitments, not every task you undertake has the same impact on your overall goals. For example, a business owner might discover that a small percentage of their clients account for the majority of revenue. Similarly, a student might realize that focusing on a few key study methods leads to the majority of exam success. The challenge lies in identifying these high-impact areas and redirecting your efforts toward them.

One practical way to begin is through data and observation. Keep track of your activities and their outcomes over a set period. This could mean logging how you spend your work hours, noting the results of various tasks, or even reflecting on moments when you feel most productive or effective. For instance, someone trying to grow a social media presence might analyze which types of posts generate the most engagement and focus on creating similar content. Patterns will emerge, revealing the activities that yield the greatest results. Identifying these patterns is the first step in applying the 80/20 Principle to your life.

Once you've pinpointed the critical 20%, the next step is to eliminate or delegate the less impactful 80%. This can feel counterintuitive, especially if you've been conditioned to equate busyness with productivity. However, freeing yourself from low-value tasks creates space for deeper focus and effort on the areas that truly matter. For instance, if responding to non-urgent emails consumes a significant portion of your day but contributes little to your long-term goals, consider setting aside specific times to address them or delegating the task entirely. Similarly, in a team setting, delegating repetitive or administrative tasks to others allows you to concentrate on high-priority initiatives.

Applying the 80/20 Principle also requires a willingness to say no. Opportunities and demands are endless, but time and energy are finite. Learning to prioritize the critical few often means declining the trivial many. For example, a professional striving to complete a major project might need to turn down invitations to unrelated meetings or social events that don't align with their immediate priorities. Saying no can be uncomfortable, especially when it involves turning down requests from colleagues or loved ones, but it's a necessary skill for maintaining focus and achieving meaningful results. The clarity gained by focusing on the most impactful activities far outweighs the discomfort of setting boundaries.

The Pareto Principle extends beyond individual tasks to broader goals and strategies. It prompts you to question whether the goals you're pursuing are themselves aligned with your values and aspirations. Often, people expend significant effort chasing objectives that, even if achieved, contribute little to their overall happiness or success. Applying the 80/20 Principle at this level means asking tough questions about what truly matters to you and aligning your efforts accordingly. For instance, someone working long hours to climb the corporate ladder might realize that their true goal is financial independence, prompting them to explore alternative career paths or investment opportunities that align more closely with this vision.

The principle is equally applicable in personal relationships and social interactions. Not all connections have the same depth or influence on your well-being. Focusing on the relationships that provide the most support, joy, or growth can enhance your personal life just as much as it can your professional endeavors. For example, instead of spreading yourself thin by maintaining superficial ties with a large number of acquaintances, you might choose to invest more time in nurturing a few close friendships or family bonds that are genuinely fulfilling.

The 80/20 Principle also encourages you to consider the quality of your efforts rather than just the quantity. Working smarter, not harder, becomes the mantra. For instance, instead of spending hours perfecting every detail of a presentation, identify the key points that will resonate most with your audience and focus your energy there. The same applies to learning new skills or acquiring knowledge. Rather than attempting to master every aspect of a subject, concentrate on the core concepts or techniques that will deliver the greatest results. This targeted approach accelerates progress and reduces the likelihood of feeling overwhelmed.

One of the most powerful aspects of the 80/20 Principle is its ability to simplify complexity. Modern life is often inundated with options, distractions, and competing priorities. The principle acts as a filter, helping you cut through the noise to focus on what truly moves the needle. For instance, an entrepreneur developing a new product might be tempted to incorporate every feature imaginable, but focusing on the few features that address the most significant customer needs can lead to a more successful launch. This process of simplification not only clarifies your direction but also makes it easier to communicate your priorities to others.

While the 80/20 Principle is a powerful tool, it's not a one-size-fits-all solution. Its application requires nuance and ongoing evaluation. What constitutes the critical 20% can change over time as circumstances, goals, and priorities evolve. Regularly revisiting your activities and their outcomes ensures that you remain aligned with what matters most. For instance, a writer who initially focused on building a following through social media might later shift their focus to producing high-quality content as their audience grows. Flexibility and adaptability are essential for maintaining the principle's effectiveness.

Critics of the 80/20 Principle sometimes argue that it oversimplifies complex systems or undervalues the importance of less glamorous tasks. While it's true that not every activity can be streamlined or delegated, the principle is not about ignoring the 80% entirely. Rather, it's about ensuring that the majority of your time and energy is directed toward the areas that yield the greatest impact. For example, while a business owner might spend most of their time developing growth strategies, they still need to ensure that routine operations run smoothly, even if those tasks are delegated to others. Balancing the principle with practical realities ensures that nothing essential falls through the cracks.

Chapter 9: The Intersection of Discipline and Flexibility

Adapting When Plans Go Awry

Life rarely unfolds exactly as planned. No matter how carefully you map out your ambitions, setbacks, surprises, and unforeseen obstacles have a way of creeping in, disrupting even the most well-organized plans. While this unpredictability can feel disheartening, it is also an inevitable part of the human experience. The ability to adapt when things go awry is not a sign of weakness or failure but a testament to resilience and resourcefulness. Developing this skill allows you to navigate challenges with confidence, maintaining momentum even when the path forward feels uncertain.

The first step in adapting when plans fall apart is acknowledging the situation without spiraling into frustration or self-blame. It's easy to get caught up in a cycle of "what ifs" and "if onlys," but dwelling on what you can't change wastes valuable energy. Instead, take a moment to assess the reality of the situation. What has changed? What new obstacles have presented themselves? At this stage, clarity is key. For example, if a project deadline gets moved up unexpectedly, rather than lamenting lost time, shift your focus to understanding the new parameters. What resources do you still have? What aspects of the original plan can be salvaged or adjusted? This grounded perspective is the foundation of effective problem-solving.

Once you've assessed the situation, it's important to recalibrate your expectations. Plans that once seemed achievable may now need to be scaled back, restructured, or even postponed. This can feel like a setback, but flexibility is crucial for long-term success. Adapting doesn't mean giving up on your goals; it means finding new ways to approach them. For instance, if you're training for a marathon but sustain an injury, you might shift your focus from running to cross-training activities that maintain your fitness while you recover. Adjusting your approach ensures that progress continues, even if it looks different from what you initially envisioned.

Creativity often plays a pivotal role in adaptation. When the original path is blocked, finding an alternative requires thinking outside the box. This might involve exploring unconventional solutions, seeking input from others, or taking inspiration from unexpected sources. Consider the story of a small business owner whose supplier unexpectedly goes out of business. Rather than panic, they might use the disruption as an opportunity to research local suppliers, ultimately discovering a more cost-effective and reliable partnership. Challenges frequently carry hidden opportunities, but uncovering them requires a willingness to experiment and innovate.

Another key aspect of adapting is prioritizing what matters most. When circumstances change, not everything on your original to-do list will hold the same level of importance. Reassess your priorities in light of the new reality, focusing on high-impact tasks that align with your core goals. For example, a student facing a sudden change in their exam schedule might decide to concentrate their study efforts on their weakest subjects rather than trying to cover everything at once. This strategic shift ensures that your energy is directed where it will have the greatest effect, minimizing wasted effort.

Communication is often an overlooked but essential component of adapting to unexpected changes. When plans go off course, it's important to keep stakeholders, collaborators, or supporters informed. Clear and honest communication can prevent misunderstandings, build trust, and even generate support or solutions you hadn't considered. For instance, if a team project hits an unexpected roadblock, updating your colleagues promptly allows everyone to contribute ideas and adjust their roles as needed. Transparency fosters a sense of shared responsibility, making it easier to navigate challenges collectively.

Emotional resilience is equally critical when dealing with disruptions. Changing plans can evoke feelings of disappointment, frustration, or even fear, particularly when the stakes are high. While these emotions are natural, they can cloud judgment if left unchecked. Developing emotional resilience involves acknowledging your feelings without letting them dictate your actions. Practices like mindfulness, journaling, or simply taking a moment to breathe can help you regain composure and approach the situation with a clear mind. For example, an entrepreneur facing an unexpected financial setback might take a day to process their emotions before regrouping to develop a revised budget or business strategy. Emotional resilience doesn't eliminate challenges, but it equips you to face them with greater clarity and determination.

Seeking support is another powerful strategy for navigating unexpected changes. No one achieves success in isolation, and leaning on your network during challenging times can provide fresh perspectives, encouragement, and practical assistance. Whether it's a mentor offering advice, a friend lending a listening ear, or a colleague stepping in to share the workload, support systems are invaluable when plans go awry. For instance, a parent juggling work and childcare after a sudden school closure might turn to family members or trusted neighbors for help, allowing them to maintain balance during the disruption. Asking for support isn't a sign of weakness; it's a testament to your resourcefulness and ability to collaborate.

One of the most important lessons in adapting is learning to let go of perfectionism. When circumstances change, clinging to an idealized version of your original plan can hinder progress. Instead, embrace the idea that "good enough" is often sufficient to move forward. For example, if an artist's original vision for a project becomes unfeasible due to time constraints, simplifying the concept or focusing on key elements can still produce a meaningful result. Letting go of rigid expectations allows you to focus on what's achievable, rather than getting stuck in what's no longer possible.

Reflection is a vital part of the adaptation process. Once you've navigated a disruption, take the time to evaluate what worked, what didn't, and what you've learned. This reflection not only helps you process the experience but also prepares you for future challenges. For example, a traveler whose trip is disrupted by flight cancellations might reflect on the value of travel insurance or the importance of packing essentials in a carry-on bag. These insights can inform future plans, making you more resilient and adaptable over time.

Finally, remember that adapting isn't just about reacting to change; it's about growing through it. Disruptions have a way of revealing strengths, uncovering opportunities, and fostering resilience in ways that smooth sailing never could. For instance, a writer who loses their draft due to a technical glitch might discover that rewriting the piece leads to a stronger, more refined version. Challenges test your limits, but they also expand them, leaving you better equipped to handle whatever comes next.

Striking the Balance Between Rigidity and Growth

Life is an intricate dance between structure and flexibility. On one hand, the need for order and routine offers stability and a sense of control. On the other, the inevitability of growth and change demands adaptability and openness. Striking the balance between these two forces is one of the most nuanced and rewarding challenges we face. Too much rigidity can stifle creativity, limit opportunities, and make us resistant to necessary change. Conversely, an excess of flexibility can lead to chaos, lack of direction, and a failure to meet long-term objectives. The key lies in cultivating a dynamic equilibrium, where structure supports growth and growth, in turn, refines and enhances structure.

The human tendency to cling to rigidity often stems from a fear of the unknown. Familiar routines and established norms provide comfort, creating the illusion of control in an unpredictable world. While this sense of security is valuable, it can become a double-edged sword when it prevents us from stepping beyond our comfort zones or adapting to changing circumstances. For example, a professional who insists on sticking to outdated methods, despite advancements in their field, risks falling behind peers who embrace innovation. Similarly, personal relationships can stagnate when individuals resist growth, holding onto patterns of behavior that no longer serve them or their loved ones.

Rigid structures, however, are not inherently problematic. In fact, they form the backbone of many successful endeavors. Consider the daily routines of high-performing individuals, such as athletes or entrepreneurs. Their schedules are often meticulously planned, with dedicated time for training, work, rest, and reflection. These routines create a framework that supports their goals, ensuring consistency and minimizing distractions. Without such structure, the pursuit of excellence would be far more challenging. But even within these highly regimented routines, there is room for flexibility. An athlete recovering from an injury, for instance, must adjust their training regimen to accommodate their body's needs, demonstrating that growth often requires deviation from the norm.

Growth, by its very nature, is fluid and unpredictable. It often involves venturing into uncharted territory, experimenting with new approaches, and embracing the discomfort of not knowing exactly what comes next. This can feel unsettling for those who prefer the certainty of a fixed plan. However, growth and adaptability are essential for long-term success, both personally and professionally. Businesses that fail to innovate in response to market changes often find themselves obsolete, while individuals who resist personal growth may struggle to evolve in ways that fulfill their potential. For instance, someone who avoids learning new skills out of a fear of failure may miss out on career opportunities or personal enrichment.

The interplay between structure and growth becomes especially apparent in goal setting. A rigid approach to goals might involve creating a detailed plan and adhering to it without deviation, even when circumstances shift. While this approach can foster discipline, it often fails to account for the realities of life, where unexpected challenges and opportunities arise. On the other hand, a purely growth-oriented approach might involve setting broad, undefined goals, relying on spontaneity to shape the path forward. This can lead to a lack of focus, as the absence of structure makes it difficult to measure progress or stay on track. The optimal approach lies somewhere in the middle: setting clear, actionable goals while remaining open to revising them as needed.

For example, imagine an aspiring writer who sets a goal to complete a novel in one year. A rigid approach might involve allocating specific word counts to each day and refusing to deviate from this schedule, even if it leads to burnout or compromises the quality of their work. A growth-oriented approach, on the other hand, might involve writing whenever inspiration strikes, without a clear plan or timeline, potentially resulting in a half-finished manuscript. By balancing structure with flexibility, the writer could establish a consistent writing habit while allowing room for creativity and adjustments along the way.

One practical way to strike this balance is by adopting a mindset of "structured flexibility." This involves creating a framework that provides direction and consistency while leaving room for adaptation and growth. For instance, a professional might use time blocking to structure their workday, dedicating blocks of time to specific tasks or categories. Within these blocks, however, they allow themselves the freedom to prioritize based on current needs or unexpected developments. This approach ensures that essential tasks are addressed without feeling overly constrained by a fixed schedule.

Another valuable strategy is to actively seek feedback and reflection. Growth often requires stepping outside of your own perspective and considering how others perceive your actions, goals, or methods. Constructive feedback can reveal blind spots, challenge assumptions, and provide insights that lead to meaningful change. For example, a manager who regularly solicits feedback from their team can identify areas where their leadership style might be too rigid or where more structure could benefit the group. Reflecting on this feedback allows them to make adjustments that enhance both their own growth and the effectiveness of their team.

The ability to balance structure and growth also hinges on self-awareness. Understanding your natural tendencies—whether you lean toward rigidity or flexibility—can help you develop strategies to counterbalance these inclinations. For instance, someone who thrives on routine but struggles with change might practice intentionally stepping outside their comfort zone, such as trying a new hobby or taking on a challenging project. Conversely, someone who prefers spontaneity might work on establishing small, consistent habits, like setting a regular bedtime or creating a weekly meal plan. These intentional actions help develop the skills needed to navigate both structure and growth with greater ease.

It's important to recognize that the balance between rigidity and growth is not static. Different phases of life, projects, or goals may require different approaches. For example, the early stages of launching a business might demand a high degree of flexibility as you adapt to market feedback and refine your offerings. Once the business is established, however, implementing structured processes becomes essential for scaling and maintaining quality. Similarly, personal growth often involves cycles of exploration and consolidation, where periods of experimentation are followed by moments of reflection and integration.

Chapter 10: The Discipline of Saying No

Setting Boundaries Without Guilt

Boundaries are the invisible lines that define where your needs, responsibilities, and priorities end and someone else's begin. They are an essential foundation for healthy relationships, personal well-being, and a balanced life. Yet, setting and maintaining boundaries often feels like a daunting task, especially when guilt begins to creep in. Many people struggle to assert their limits because they fear disappointing others, being perceived as selfish, or jeopardizing their relationships. Overcoming this guilt requires not only a shift in mindset but also a clear understanding of why boundaries are necessary and how they ultimately benefit everyone involved.

Boundaries are not a form of rejection or selfishness but rather an act of self-respect and mutual respect. Without them, you risk overcommitting, burning out, and feeling resentful toward others. Imagine a friend who constantly asks for your help with projects but never reciprocates when you need support. If you continue to say yes, despite feeling overwhelmed, you may harbor frustration that eventually damages the friendship. Setting a boundary in this scenario—such as explaining your limits and declining when you're too busy—allows you to protect your energy while maintaining honesty in the relationship. Far from being harmful, boundaries preserve your emotional and mental health, ensuring you can show up for others in meaningful ways.

The first step to setting boundaries without guilt is identifying where they are needed. This often involves reflecting on areas of your life where you feel stretched too thin, taken advantage of, or consistently uncomfortable. Pay attention to patterns. Do you find yourself agreeing to last-minute plans that disrupt your schedule? Are there people in your life who expect constant availability, regardless of your own needs? These are signs that your boundaries may be too loose or undefined. By pinpointing the areas where you feel drained or frustrated, you can begin to clarify what limits would help restore balance.

Once you've identified where boundaries are needed, the next step is determining what those boundaries look like. This requires honest self-assessment. What are your non-negotiables? For instance, if you need uninterrupted time to focus on a project, you might set a boundary around answering work emails after a certain hour. If you value quality time with family, you may limit social obligations that interfere with that priority. Boundaries are deeply personal and should align with your values, goals, and well-being. They are not about controlling others but about defining what you can and cannot accommodate.

Communicating your boundaries effectively is one of the most challenging yet crucial aspects of the process. Clear, assertive communication minimizes misunderstandings and ensures that your intentions are respected. Avoid vague statements or apologetic language, as these can undermine the strength of your boundary. For example, instead of saying, "I'm sorry, I think I might not be able to help you this time," try, "I won't be able to help with this because I need to focus on other priorities." The former leaves room for negotiation and conveys hesitation, while the latter is direct and confident. Remember, you're not asking for permission to set boundaries—you're stating them.

Anticipating pushback is a critical part of preparing to enforce boundaries. Not everyone will immediately accept or understand your limits, especially if they've benefited from your lack of boundaries in the past. For instance, a coworker who is used to you taking on extra tasks may react with surprise or disappointment when you begin saying no. While this reaction can trigger guilt, it's important to remember that their feelings are not your responsibility. Boundaries are about taking care of yourself, not managing others' emotions. Stay firm but empathetic, reiterating your limits without becoming defensive or apologetic.

It's also essential to recognize that guilt is a natural response when setting boundaries, especially if you're accustomed to prioritizing others' needs over your own. Society often reinforces the notion that self-sacrifice is virtuous, leading many to equate setting limits with selfishness. However, this perspective is flawed. Boundaries are not about depriving others but about ensuring that you have the capacity to give in healthy, sustainable ways. Reframing your mindset can help alleviate guilt. Instead of viewing boundaries as walls, think of them as bridges—structures that facilitate healthier, more balanced connections.

Practicing self-compassion is another powerful tool for managing guilt. Remind yourself that your needs are valid and that it's impossible to please everyone. You have the right to prioritize your well-being without feeling ashamed or apologetic. For example, if you decline an invitation to an event because you need rest, acknowledge that this decision honors your health and energy. Self-compassion involves treating yourself with the same kindness and understanding that you would offer a friend in a similar situation. It reinforces the idea that setting boundaries is an act of self-care, not selfishness.

Boundaries also require consistency. While it's tempting to make exceptions or bend your limits to avoid conflict, doing so undermines their effectiveness. Imagine setting a boundary with a friend who frequently calls late at night, disrupting your sleep. If you answer their calls occasionally despite having expressed your need for rest, you send mixed signals, making it harder for them to respect your limit. Consistency reinforces your boundaries and demonstrates that they are non-negotiable. It also builds trust, as others learn to rely on your clear and predictable communication.

Over time, setting and maintaining boundaries becomes easier as you develop confidence in your ability to uphold them. This confidence grows with practice and positive reinforcement. For example, you might notice that saying no to unnecessary obligations frees up time for activities that truly matter to you, enhancing your overall well-being. Similarly, relationships often improve when boundaries are respected, as both parties feel more secure and understood. These outcomes reinforce the value of boundaries, motivating you to continue prioritizing them.

Boundaries are not static; they evolve as your needs, circumstances, and relationships change. Periodically reassessing your boundaries ensures that they remain relevant and effective. For instance, a boundary that was necessary during a particularly busy season of life may no longer be needed once your schedule lightens. Conversely, new challenges may require the establishment of additional limits. Flexibility in adjusting your boundaries demonstrates self-awareness and adaptability, allowing you to navigate life's complexities with greater ease.

Protecting Your Energy for What Truly Matters

Energy is one of the most valuable resources you have, yet it is often treated as though it's limitless. Each day, countless demands compete for your attention, draining you of mental, emotional, and physical reserves. From work obligations to social expectations, the tug-of-war for your energy can leave you feeling depleted, overwhelmed, and disconnected from the things that matter most. Protecting your energy is not about shutting out the world or avoiding responsibilities—it's about making deliberate choices to focus on what truly aligns with your values, priorities, and goals. When you learn to safeguard your energy effectively, you gain the clarity and strength to invest in the aspects of life that bring you fulfillment and purpose.

The first step in protecting your energy is understanding where it currently goes. Many people move through their days on autopilot, unaware of how much time and energy they expend on tasks, people, or situations that offer little in return. Take stock of your daily routines and interactions. Are there activities that consistently leave you feeling drained or unmotivated? Do certain relationships feel more like obligations than genuine connections? Identifying these energy drains is crucial because it allows you to pinpoint areas where boundaries, adjustments, or eliminations are needed. For instance, scrolling through social media for hours might seem harmless, but it can sap your mental energy and leave you feeling scattered or dissatisfied. Similarly, agreeing to every social invitation out of politeness can consume emotional reserves that could be better spent on meaningful relationships.

Once you've identified the energy drains in your life, the next step is to prioritize. Not everything that demands your attention deserves it, and not every task is equally important. Learning to distinguish between what is essential and what is expendable is a skill that can transform how you allocate your energy. Begin by defining your core values and goals. What truly matters to you? Perhaps it's your family, your personal growth, a creative passion, or a professional endeavor. These priorities serve as your compass, guiding you toward activities and commitments that align with your purpose. When you have a clear sense of what matters most, it becomes easier to say no to distractions, obligations, or opportunities that don't align with your values.

Saying no is one of the most powerful tools for protecting your energy, yet it's also one of the hardest to wield. Many people feel an intense pressure to say yes, whether out of fear of disappointing others, a desire to be helpful, or a reluctance to miss out. However, every yes you give to something unimportant is a no to something that truly matters. Learning to say no with confidence requires a shift in perspective. It's not about rejecting people or shirking responsibilities—it's about honoring your own limits and making space for what truly deserves your energy. For example, declining a last-minute work request that interferes with your family dinner is not an act of defiance; it's a choice to prioritize connection and balance. Saying no doesn't have to be harsh or confrontational—it can be done with kindness and clarity, reinforcing your boundaries without alienating others.

Another key strategy for protecting your energy is managing your environment. The spaces you inhabit—both physical and digital—play a significant role in how you feel and function. A cluttered workspace, for instance, can create mental chaos, making it harder to focus and stay productive. Similarly, constant notifications from your phone or email can fragment your attention, leaving you mentally exhausted by the end of the day. Take control of your environment by creating spaces that support your well-being and productivity. This might involve decluttering your home, setting up a dedicated work area, or turning off non-essential notifications during focused tasks. A supportive environment acts as a buffer against unnecessary energy drains, allowing you to channel your efforts more effectively.

Protecting your energy also requires cultivating habits that replenish it. Just as you wouldn't drive a car without refueling it, you can't expect to function at your best without regularly recharging your mental, emotional, and physical reserves. Self-care is not a luxury; it's a necessity. This includes basics like getting enough sleep, eating nourishing foods, and engaging in regular physical activity. But self-care goes beyond physical needs—it also involves nurturing your emotional and mental well-being. Practices like mindfulness, journaling, or spending time in nature can help you reconnect with yourself and regain a sense of balance. For instance, taking a 15-minute walk outside during a stressful workday can clear your mind and restore your focus, allowing you to approach tasks with renewed energy.

Relationships are another critical factor in protecting your energy. The people you surround yourself with have a profound impact on how you feel and function. Some relationships uplift and energize you, while others drain and deplete you. It's important to evaluate the dynamics of your social circle and take steps to cultivate connections that align with your values and priorities. This doesn't mean cutting people out of your life indiscriminately—it means being intentional about where and with whom you invest your energy. For example, spending time with a friend who listens, supports, and inspires you is far more valuable than engaging in superficial interactions that leave you feeling empty. By fostering meaningful relationships, you create a network of support that sustains and enriches you.

Time management is another essential aspect of protecting your energy. How you use your time directly impacts how much energy you have for the things that matter most. Poor time management often leads to feelings of overwhelm, as you struggle to juggle competing demands without clear priorities. To regain control, start by identifying your most productive hours—those times of day when your energy and focus are at their peak. Use these periods for high-priority tasks that require your full attention, and reserve less critical activities for times when your energy naturally wanes. Additionally, consider implementing techniques like batching similar tasks together or using time-blocking to structure your day. These strategies can help you work more efficiently, reducing mental fatigue and freeing up energy for other pursuits.

Emotional resilience is another important component of energy protection. Life is filled with challenges and setbacks that can drain your emotional reserves if left unchecked. Developing resilience allows you to navigate these difficulties without becoming overwhelmed or discouraged. This involves cultivating a mindset of acceptance and adaptability, recognizing that not everything is within your control. For instance, when faced with an unexpected obstacle, focusing on what you can do rather than dwelling on what you can't helps you conserve energy and maintain momentum. Emotional resilience also involves practicing gratitude, which shifts your focus from what's lacking to what's abundant in your life.

Gratitude fosters a sense of positivity and perspective, replenishing your emotional energy even in the face of challenges.

Finally, protecting your energy requires ongoing self-awareness and reflection. Your needs and priorities will evolve over time, and what drains or replenishes your energy may change as well. Regularly check in with yourself to assess how you're feeling and whether your current habits, relationships, and commitments align with your values. This might involve journaling, meditating, or simply taking a few moments each day to reflect on what's working and what isn't. By staying attuned to your own needs, you can make adjustments as necessary, ensuring that your energy remains focused on what truly matters.

Chapter 11: Tracking, Measuring, and Adjusting Your Progress

The Importance of Self-Reflection and Feedback

Self-reflection and feedback are two of the most powerful tools for personal growth and self-awareness. They function as mirrors, revealing truths about our actions, decisions, and behaviors that might otherwise remain hidden. In a world that constantly pushes us to move forward, faster and faster, it's easy to neglect the practice of looking inward and seeking external perspectives. Yet, without these practices, progress can become aimless, growth stagnant, and patterns of behavior unexamined. The importance of self-reflection and feedback lies in their ability to foster clarity, accountability, and a deeper understanding of oneself and one's environment.

Self-reflection begins with the act of pausing. It is the deliberate decision to step back from the noise of daily life and examine your thoughts, emotions, and actions with honesty and curiosity. Many people avoid self-reflection because it can feel uncomfortable, even confronting. It requires facing your mistakes, acknowledging where you've fallen short, and accepting parts of yourself that you might rather ignore. But within this discomfort lies the opportunity for transformation. By identifying what is working, what isn't, and why, you can make intentional changes that align your actions with your values and goals.

One of the simplest yet most effective ways to practice self-reflection is through journaling. Writing down your thoughts and experiences forces you to articulate them clearly, which can reveal patterns and insights that might otherwise go unnoticed. Consider a person who feels constantly overwhelmed at work. By journaling about their daily routines, they might discover that they're overcommitting to tasks out of a fear of disappointing others. This realization is a pivotal moment of self-awareness, one that enables them to make conscious choices about how to set boundaries and prioritize their workload. The act of writing creates a tangible record of your reflections, allowing you to track your growth over time and revisit lessons learned.

Another valuable technique is to use guided questions as prompts for self-reflection. These questions might include: What did I do well today? What challenges did I face, and how did I respond? What could I have done differently? What emotions am I feeling, and what might be causing them? These questions encourage you to move beyond surface-level thinking and dig deeper into the motivations, fears, and beliefs that drive your actions. Over time, this practice sharpens your ability to identify not only what you want to change but also the underlying reasons for those changes.

While self-reflection is an inward-facing practice, feedback represents its outward counterpart. Feedback involves seeking input from others to gain perspectives that you might not be able to see on your own. We all have blind spots—areas where our self-perception doesn't align with how others experience us. These blind spots can be both strengths and weaknesses, and feedback is the key to uncovering them. For example, you might believe you're an effective communicator because you articulate your ideas clearly, but a colleague might point out that you often interrupt others during discussions. This feedback, though potentially difficult to hear, provides an opportunity to grow and improve in a way that self-reflection alone might not reveal.

The quality of feedback depends largely on the source and the context in which it is given. It's important to seek feedback from individuals whose opinions you trust and respect, whether they are mentors, colleagues, friends, or family members. These are the people who have your best interests at heart and are more likely to provide constructive, actionable insights rather than criticism that is rooted in bias or negativity. Additionally, the way you ask for feedback matters. Instead of vague questions like, "How am I doing?" ask specific ones, such as, "How do you think I could improve my presentation skills?" or "Is there anything I could do differently to better support the team?" Specificity invites clarity and actionable responses, making the feedback more useful.

Receiving feedback gracefully is a skill in itself. It's natural to feel defensive or even hurt when confronted with critiques, but it's crucial to approach feedback with an open mind and a willingness to learn. One way to manage this is by separating the feedback from your sense of self-worth. Receiving constructive criticism does not mean you are a failure; it means there is room for growth. For instance, if a manager points out that you need to be more organized in your project planning, resist the urge to justify or dismiss their observation. Instead, thank them for their input, reflect on their perspective, and consider how you might implement their suggestions. Feedback is not a personal attack—it's a gift that helps you improve.

Balancing self-reflection and feedback creates a more holistic approach to self-awareness. Self-reflection allows you to assess your internal landscape—your thoughts, feelings, and motivations—while feedback provides external validation or challenge to those assessments. Together, they create a feedback loop of growth. Imagine an employee who sets a personal goal to be more collaborative at work. Through self-reflection, they identify moments when they could have sought input from colleagues but chose to work independently out of a desire to maintain control. They then seek feedback from their team members, who confirm that they'd appreciate more opportunities to contribute. This combination of internal and external insights enables the employee to take meaningful steps toward becoming a more collaborative team player.

However, it's important to recognize that both self-reflection and feedback can be misused or misunderstood. Self-reflection, for instance, can easily slip into rumination—endlessly replaying your mistakes or shortcomings without taking action to address them. This kind of over-analysis can be paralyzing, leading to self-doubt and inaction. To avoid this, focus on framing your reflections in a constructive way. Instead of dwelling on what went wrong, ask yourself what you can learn from the experience and how you can apply that lesson moving forward.

Similarly, feedback can become counterproductive if it is not given or received in the right spirit. Feedback that is overly critical, vague, or unsolicited can feel more like an attack than an opportunity for growth. On the receiving end, it's essential to filter feedback, discerning which insights are valuable and which might stem from the giver's biases or misunderstandings. Not all feedback is worth acting on, and developing the discernment to differentiate between helpful and unhelpful input is a crucial skill.

Effective Tools and Techniques for Measuring Success

Measuring success is a practice that goes far beyond ticking off tasks on a to-do list or reaching arbitrary milestones. It's about understanding what progress means to you, how it aligns with your goals, and how to evaluate it meaningfully. For many, success feels elusive because it's either poorly defined or measured in ways that don't resonate with their personal values. The tools and techniques for measuring success are essential because they provide clarity, structure, and insights that help you stay on track and recalibrate when needed.

The starting point for any meaningful measurement is defining what success looks like in a specific context. This definition must be personal, precise, and rooted in your priorities. Without clarity, you risk adopting generic benchmarks that may not align with your actual objectives. For example, someone pursuing a healthier lifestyle might initially consider weight loss as the primary measure of success. However, upon reflection, they might realize that improved energy levels, better sleep, and increased strength are more meaningful indicators of progress. By identifying what truly matters, you create a foundation for measuring success in ways that feel authentic and motivating.

Once you've clarified your personal definition of success, setting measurable goals becomes the next step. Vague goals such as "I want to be better at my job" or "I want to improve my relationships" lack the specificity needed to track progress effectively. Instead, break down these aspirations into concrete, actionable objectives. For instance, "I want to be better at my job" could translate into measurable goals like completing a professional certification within six months, increasing sales by 15% in the next quarter, or receiving positive feedback from a manager during the next performance review. These specific targets provide clear benchmarks against which you can evaluate your progress.

One of the most widely used frameworks for goal-setting and measuring success is the SMART criteria: Specific, Measurable, Achievable, Relevant, and Time-bound. This approach ensures that your goals are not only clear but also realistic and aligned with your broader objectives. For example, if you're looking to build a new skill, a SMART goal might be: "Complete an online coding course and develop a small application within three months." This goal is specific (coding course and application), measurable (completion and functionality), achievable (assuming prior basics), relevant (to a career or personal interest), and time-bound (three months). The SMART framework simplifies the process of translating abstract aspirations into actionable plans.

Tracking progress is equally important when measuring success. Without a system for monitoring your efforts, it's easy to lose sight of how far you've come or whether you're drifting off course. Keeping a journal, using apps, or maintaining spreadsheets can help you document milestones and setbacks along the way. For instance, if you're saving money for a major purchase, tracking your savings in a spreadsheet allows you to see incremental progress and adjust your spending habits if necessary. Similarly, if you're trying to develop a habit, apps like habit trackers can provide visual representations of your consistency, reinforcing your commitment.

Feedback is another invaluable tool for measuring success. While self-assessment is important, external perspectives can reveal blind spots or validate your progress in ways you might not notice on your own. Seeking feedback from mentors, colleagues, friends, or family members allows you to gauge how your efforts are perceived by others. For example, if your goal is to improve public speaking, recording your speeches and sharing them with trusted individuals for critique can provide constructive insights that propel your improvement. Feedback also serves as a reality check, ensuring that your perception of success aligns with observable outcomes.

Milestones play a crucial role in sustaining motivation and measuring success over time. Long-term goals can often feel overwhelming or unattainable, but breaking them into smaller, manageable milestones makes the journey more tangible. For instance, if you're working toward running a marathon, setting interim goals like running a 5K, then a 10K, and eventually a half-marathon creates a sense of achievement at each stage. Celebrating these smaller victories reinforces your progress and keeps you motivated to continue. Milestones also provide opportunities for reflection and adjustment, allowing you to refine your strategies as you move closer to your ultimate objective.

Quantitative metrics, while valuable, are not the only way to measure success. Qualitative assessments often reveal nuances that numbers cannot capture. For example, someone building a career might use metrics like salary increases or promotions as indicators of success. However, qualitative measures such as job satisfaction, work-life balance, or the impact of their contributions can provide a fuller picture of their progress. Combining quantitative and qualitative evaluations ensures that you're not solely focused on surface-level achievements but are also considering the deeper, more personal aspects of success.

Time audits are another effective technique for measuring success, particularly when it comes to productivity and time management. A time audit involves tracking how you spend your hours over a given period and comparing it to your priorities. For example, if your goal is to write a novel, but a time audit reveals that you're only spending five hours a month on writing while dedicating 20 hours to non-essential activities, it's a clear signal that adjustments are needed. Time audits highlight discrepancies between your intentions and actions, providing actionable insights that help you realign your efforts with your goals.

Visual tools like mind maps, vision boards, or progress charts can also enhance your ability to measure success. These tools provide a visual representation of your goals, progress, and aspirations, making them more tangible and easier to track. For example, a vision board filled with images and quotes that represent your desired outcomes can serve as a daily reminder of what you're working toward. Similarly, creating a progress chart for a fitness goal, where you record each workout or improvement, can provide a sense of accomplishment and keep you motivated to continue.

Regularly reviewing and reassessing your goals is essential to ensure that your definition of success evolves with your changing circumstances and priorities. Life is dynamic, and what once seemed important may lose relevance over time. For instance, a professional goal you set five years ago might no longer align with your current career aspirations. Periodic reviews allow you to refine your objectives, celebrate progress, and make informed decisions about where to focus your energy moving forward. This practice ensures that your efforts remain purposeful and aligned with your values.

The emotional aspect of measuring success should not be overlooked. Success is not just about achieving external markers—it's also about how you feel along the way. Do you feel energized and fulfilled by your progress, or are you constantly stressed and dissatisfied? Emotional check-ins help you gauge whether your pursuit of success is enhancing your well-being or detracting from it. For example, if you're working toward a promotion but find that the process is causing burnout and straining your relationships, it might be worth reevaluating whether the goal is worth the cost. Success should not come at the expense of your overall happiness and health.

Adaptability is another key component of measuring success. Goals and circumstances can change, and clinging rigidly to initial plans can hinder progress. For example, an entrepreneur might set a goal to launch a specific product within a year, only to discover halfway through that market conditions have shifted. In such cases, the ability to pivot and redefine success—perhaps by focusing on a different product or timeline—ensures continued progress. Flexibility allows you to respond to challenges and opportunities without losing sight of your overarching vision.

Chapter 12: The Long-Term Payoff: Discipline as a Lifestyle

The Compounding Effect of Consistent Actions

Small actions, repeated consistently over time, have the power to create monumental change. This concept, often overlooked in a culture that celebrates overnight success and dramatic transformations, is the essence of the compounding effect. At its core, the compounding effect is about understanding that progress is the result of incremental efforts building upon one another, rather than grand, singular gestures. Whether applied to personal growth, relationships, health, or career goals, consistent actions—no matter how small—are what ultimately shape the trajectory of your life.

To understand the significance of the compounding effect, consider the example of a savings account. If you deposit a modest amount of money monthly and allow it to accrue interest, over time, the growth becomes exponential. At first, the change is almost imperceptible, but as the years pass, the interest compounds, creating a snowball effect. The same principle applies to nearly every area of life. Small, meaningful actions, performed consistently, generate a momentum that is far greater than the sum of their parts. Yet, because the results often appear gradual or subtle at first, it can be challenging to trust the process and remain committed.

One of the most striking aspects of the compounding effect is how it applies to habits. A single positive habit may seem insignificant in isolation, but its long-term impact can be profound. Consider someone who commits to reading just ten pages a day. In one day, they've read a short passage. In a month, they've completed a book. In a year, they've read 12 books. Over a decade, that small daily habit has transformed them into a well-read, knowledgeable individual, potentially altering the course of their career or personal development. The beauty of this principle is that it doesn't require Herculean effort—just consistency.

Consistency, however, is where many people falter. It's easy to feel impatient when the early results of your efforts seem negligible, leading to frustration or the temptation to give up altogether. The beginning stages of any endeavor are often the most challenging because the relationship between effort and reward feels out of balance. If you start running to improve your fitness, for instance, the first few weeks may feel grueling while the physical changes remain invisible. But those early runs lay the foundation for endurance, strength, and health benefits that will bloom later. Recognizing this lag in visible results is crucial to staying the course.

The compounding effect also works in reverse, which is why it's essential to be mindful of the habits you cultivate. Negative actions or choices, repeated over time, can lead to unintended and often catastrophic consequences. A seemingly harmless habit, like buying a sugary drink every afternoon, might not have an immediate impact on your health or finances. But multiply that choice by 365 days, and suddenly you're facing potential weight gain, increased risk of health issues, and a significant dent in your wallet. Just as consistent positive actions create momentum, consistent negative actions can have a compounding effect that drags you further from your goals.

One of the most effective ways to harness the compounding effect is by setting specific, realistic goals and tracking your progress. Tracking allows you to see the accumulation of your efforts over time, which can be incredibly motivating. For instance, if your goal is to write a book, committing to writing 500 words a day might seem modest. But at the end of a month, you'll have 15,000 words—a significant portion of a manuscript. By documenting your daily progress, you create a visual representation of the compound growth, reinforcing your commitment and providing a sense of accomplishment along the way.

Another critical aspect of the compounding effect is the role of time. Time is the silent partner in this process, amplifying the impact of your efforts in ways that are often imperceptible in the short term. For this reason, patience is a fundamental virtue in leveraging the compounding effect. There will be moments when it feels like your actions aren't making a difference, when the results seem stagnant or non-existent. But time is working in your favor, even when you can't see it. Trusting that the seeds you're planting today will eventually bear fruit is the mindset required to sustain consistent action.

Relationships are another area where the compounding effect is particularly evident. Acts of kindness, understanding, and support, repeated over time, build trust and deepen bonds. A single compliment, gesture of appreciation, or moment of active listening might seem trivial, but when practiced consistently, these small actions create a foundation for meaningful and lasting connections. Conversely, neglecting to invest in relationships—through forgetfulness, selfishness, or lack of effort—can erode trust and intimacy over time. The compounding effect reminds us that relationships, like anything else, require ongoing nurturing to thrive.

One common obstacle to consistency is the tendency to focus on outcomes rather than processes. While it's natural to set goals and envision the results you want to achieve, becoming overly fixated on the end product can lead to discouragement if progress feels slow. Shifting your focus to the process itself—embracing the daily actions required to move forward—creates a sense of purpose and satisfaction that sustains you through the inevitable ups and downs. For example, instead of obsessing over losing 20 pounds, focus on enjoying your daily walk, experimenting with healthy recipes, or celebrating the energy you feel after exercising. By falling in love with the process, you're more likely to remain consistent, and the results will follow as a byproduct of your efforts.

The compounding effect also teaches the importance of starting small. Grand plans and ambitious goals often feel exciting at the outset, but they can quickly become overwhelming, leading to burnout or abandonment. Instead, begin with manageable actions that you can realistically maintain. If you're trying to establish a meditation practice, start with just one minute a day. If you want to save money, begin by setting aside a small amount each week. These small actions, while seemingly inconsequential, lay the groundwork for larger transformations. Over time, as the habit becomes ingrained, you can gradually increase the intensity or scale of your efforts.

Accountability can play a significant role in maintaining consistency and amplifying the compounding effect. Sharing your goals with a trusted friend, joining a group with similar aspirations, or hiring a coach can provide the external motivation and support needed to stay on track. Knowing that someone else is aware of your commitments adds an extra layer of accountability, making it less likely that you'll abandon your efforts. Additionally, celebrating small wins with others can reinforce your progress and keep you motivated to continue.

It's essential to periodically assess your actions to ensure that they align with your goals and values. While consistency is critical, it's equally important to ensure that the actions you're repeating are effective and meaningful. For example, if you're spending hours every day practicing a skill but aren't seeing improvement, it may be time to reevaluate your approach and adjust your methods. The compounding effect magnifies both the positive and negative, so it's vital to regularly reflect on whether your actions are moving you closer to or further from your desired outcomes.

Becoming the Best Version of Yourself

The journey to becoming the best version of yourself is deeply personal, yet universal in its appeal. It's not about perfection, nor is it a destination with a definitive endpoint. Instead, it is a continuous process of growth, self-discovery, and intentional improvement. Each individual's path is unique, shaped by their experiences, values, and aspirations. However, the principles underlying this journey are rooted in self-awareness, discipline, and a commitment to incremental progress. The best version of yourself is not someone else's ideal—it's the person you strive to be when aligned with your own purpose and potential.

Self-awareness is the foundation of any meaningful transformation. Without an honest understanding of who you are—your strengths, weaknesses, habits, and patterns—it's impossible to chart a path toward growth. Taking the time to reflect on your current state provides clarity on where you stand and highlights the areas in need of attention. It's not always an easy process. Confronting your flaws and acknowledging your limitations can feel uncomfortable, even overwhelming. But this level of honesty is crucial if you're to make lasting and meaningful change. Self-awareness allows you to set authentic goals that resonate with your true self rather than chasing aspirations imposed by society or others.

One effective method of fostering self-awareness is through mindful observation of your thoughts and behaviors. Pay attention to recurring patterns—

whether it's the way you react under stress, how you approach challenges, or the habits that dominate your day. For instance, you might notice that you often procrastinate when faced with tasks that feel daunting, or that you're quick to defensiveness when receiving feedback. These observations are not meant to be judgments but opportunities for understanding. By identifying your tendencies, you can begin to address them with intentional strategies.

Equally important is taking stock of your values and priorities. What truly matters to you? What are the principles that guide your decisions and fuel your motivation? Becoming the best version of yourself requires congruence between your actions and your values. If you value kindness, but often find yourself acting impatiently, or if you prize creativity but rarely make time for it, then there's a disconnect that needs to be addressed. Aligning your life with your values creates a sense of purpose and fulfillment that is essential in this journey.

Once you've cultivated self-awareness, the next step is to take action. Action is where intention meets reality, and it's the only way to turn aspirations into achievements. However, action without direction is futile. Setting clear, realistic goals is crucial for maintaining focus and momentum. These goals don't have to be grand or life-changing. In fact, small, achievable goals are often the most effective because they build confidence and create a sense of progress. For example, if your goal is to improve your health, start by committing to a 10-minute walk each day. Over time, this small habit can evolve into a more comprehensive fitness routine.

Discipline is the glue that holds this process together. While motivation can spark the desire for change, discipline ensures that you follow through, even when motivation wanes. It's easy to feel inspired at the beginning of a journey, but sustaining that effort over weeks, months, or years requires a deeper commitment. Discipline is about showing up, day after day, regardless of how you feel in the moment. It's about prioritizing long-term gains over short-term comforts. For instance, the discipline to wake up early and dedicate time to a personal project might feel inconvenient in the moment, but it's an investment in your future self.

Embracing failure as a natural part of growth is another essential component of becoming the best version of yourself. Too often, people view failure as evidence of inadequacy, rather than as an opportunity to learn and refine their approach. The truth is, failure is inevitable on the path to self-improvement. Whether it's a missed goal, a setback in progress, or an unexpected obstacle, these moments are valuable opportunities to build resilience and adaptability. Each failure holds a lesson—about what works, what doesn't, and how you can adjust moving forward. For example, if you set a goal to write every day but find yourself falling behind, reflect on the barriers preventing consistency. Perhaps your schedule needs adjustment, or your expectations need to be more realistic.

Surrounding yourself with supportive individuals can significantly impact your progress. The people in your life play a powerful role in shaping your mindset, habits, and opportunities. Seek out relationships that inspire, challenge, and uplift you. This doesn't mean avoiding constructive criticism—in fact, feedback from trusted individuals can be invaluable. However, it's important to distance yourself from relationships that drain your energy or undermine your efforts. A friend who constantly criticizes your ambitions or a colleague who dismisses your ideas can hinder your growth. On the other hand, a mentor who encourages you to step outside your comfort zone or a friend who celebrates your successes can accelerate your journey.

Equally important is the relationship you cultivate with yourself. Self-compassion is a critical yet often overlooked element of personal growth. The path to becoming the best version of yourself is rarely linear, and there will be moments when you fall short of your expectations. In these moments, it's easy to spiral into self-criticism and doubt. But harsh self-judgment rarely leads to positive change. Instead, practice treating yourself with the same kindness and understanding you would offer a friend facing a similar situation. Acknowledge your efforts, forgive your mistakes, and focus on what you can do differently moving forward. Self-compassion creates the emotional resilience needed to persevere through challenges.

Celebrating progress, no matter how small, is essential for maintaining motivation and reinforcing positive behaviors. It's easy to become so focused on the end goal that you overlook the achievements along the way. But every step forward is a testament to your effort and commitment. If your goal is to learn a new language, celebrate when you master your first set of vocabulary words or hold your first conversation. If your goal is to improve your fitness, take pride in completing your first workout or reaching a new personal best. These moments of celebration remind you that progress is happening, even if the ultimate goal still feels distant.

www.ingramcontent.com/pod-product-compliance
Lightning Source LLC
Chambersburg PA
CBHW071201130726
47998CB00002B/566